New Reality

Extraordinary Living in Ordinary Life

Lisa Young

To Laurie
Love,
Lisa

ISBN 978-1-64114-174-1 (Paperback)
ISBN 978-1-64114-175-8 (Digital)

Christian Faith Publishing, Inc.
296 Chestnut Street
Meadville, PA 16335
www.christianfaithpublishing.com

Printed in the United States of America

One of the most amazing things about God was the way He redefined reality with words. God looked into chaos and spoke the hopeful words of creation. He looked into the chaos of our sin and declared us righteous in Christ. By speaking those words, coupled with our belief in them, He reconstituted our reality. If He had declared us lost He would have spoken truth, but He spoke a greater truth by recreating us with His words.

—Martin Luther, Reformer
(Sunday Sermon, 1500s)

Contents

Foreword

A line taken from Lisa Young's *New Reality* says, "Transformed life in Christ, as defined by the Bible, is a changed life from the ways of the world to a life that pleases God. This is not a superficial change by conforming to a set of external standards of behavior, but an inward spiritual renewal which manifests itself in outward actions." So many young Christians find this truth to be very difficult in the beginning stages of growing up in Christ. We tend to forget that the old us is completely gone when we accept Jesus Christ and that we have become a brand new person—a brand new being. In fact, there is nothing else like us on earth. We are a brand new creation in Christ Jesus. Being in discipleship training, I see this very often, and it is so refreshing to see how Lisa Young has captured the transformation process in her book.

Lisa says, "Truly we have been born again when we believe Jesus for salvation. We now have His nature within and can please God and walk with Him even while on earth. Very commonly, however, Christians have not yet realized their new, eternal nature." Understanding this nature in a way where we can actually walk it out is something that many do not pursue Jesus to better understand. As the pages of *New Reality* continue to unfold, Lisa describes what this walk looks like and how it may be obtained.

It is very interesting that Lisa was a student in the Discipleship School, where I am a teacher, and we endeavor to teach each student how to practically live the life that the Holy Spirit affords us. It is the life Jesus began revealing that we could have while He was on the earth, and the Holy Spirit enables us to see and do it practically. Lisa speaks about this in her work: "Our spirit is our innermost part which becomes alive to God when we receive salvation. Our human spirit is inhabited by the Holy Spirit and He renews a right spirit within us. This is the part of our being which informs everything we think, feel, say, and do." The more we understand the truth that we have been born again and begin to engage with the Holy Spirit as a Person, the more He reveals Christ as we participate and cooperate with Him in reading the Scriptures and expecting Him to answer us and show us what Christ is like in the world we live in today. There is nothing more exciting than understanding the reality of life that we have in Christ today. This is indeed the new reality that we now live in.

I am thankful for Lisa's book as I have seen her grow and come to know the Lord more fluently and to relate what she has learned with such excitement and Biblical truth. She is now one of the teachers in the Discipleship School and is passing on the keys to better understanding this new reality that we have and can enjoy in Christ as we press on to know Him better.

Larry Reese
Author and Pastor of Discipleship
Rivers Crossing Community Church

Chapter 1

New Reality

I bowed my head and was silent for a moment. A dream slowly slipping from my fingers, my heart sick, and my hope deferred. Deep longings unrealized, reality seemed to contradict the promise I was believing from God. My eyes lifted and peered at the ivory keys where such beautiful music had been created just moments before. I raised my vision to the fresh lyrics scratched haphazardly on the page resting on the piano.

> Trust Me, I know what I'm doing
> Believe Me, it's part of My plan
> Well done, good and faithful servant
> I am so pleased, I am so pleased.

Little did I know, a song I had just written would minister to me so profoundly. I felt God's presence. I felt loved. I knew He was a good Father and felt encouraged to trust Him, even in my disappointment.

Deep in the human heart is a longing to live a noteworthy life. We want to be significant, if only in our small sphere of influence. We want to know we are living for a purpose on purpose. Naturally, we all desire to move from sorrow to happiness, apathy to enjoyment, indifference to passion. Like you, I want to thrive rather than survive in a pain-ridden, stress-filled, bothersome life. I desire life to be more than it is. I desire to be more than I am.

In the Bible, God promises new life in Christ. It's the kind of life Jesus talks about in John 10:10 (NKJV) when He says, "I have come that they may have life, and that they may have it more abundantly." Other versions of the Bible talk about a rich, satisfying life—one filled with reason and fulfillment. This life has an eternal quality. It is a life marked by *more*. However, we don't have to look far to realize that many are not yet experiencing abundant life. We distance ourselves from the people and testimonies in the Bible, telling ourselves things were different when it was written. We believe that the characters were superior or that they had an unusual connection to God, so He treated them specially. Many believers are not experiencing spiritual riches like love, joy, and peace. Our lives can be just as riddled by restlessness, sin, and anxiety as the rest of the world. We are bothered by what we see on social media, concerned about violence in the news, and uncertain about the future of our nation.

When Jesus came to earth He preached the gospel of the kingdom of heaven. Both He and John the Baptist announced this kingdom is "at hand." God's kingdom is a spiritual existence now, as well as a future material manifestation. "At hand" means the kingdom of heaven is something we can grasp and draw into reality while still living on earth. Through surrendering ourselves to Jesus's lordship, we experience life in His kingdom, a life filled with the first fruits of heaven. Not only do we have hope for a glorious life with God after death, but also, we begin to experience it while here on earth. Life in God's spiritual kingdom now is a foreshadow of future life in heaven. We catch glimpses of glory when God's reality breaks into our ordinary life. This truly is extraordinary!

God's intention is to walk with His creation in close communion; He desires to "do life" with us. When He created Adam and Eve, He intended to help and teach them every day in the Garden of Eden. But they chose their own way and thus began the separation between God and man. When Jesus came to earth, He showed us how to do life with God in perfect unison. By becoming the final sacrifice and offering eternal salvation, He opened the door for us to experience life with God as it once was in the garden. Romans 8:1–2 (NLT) says, "So now there is no condemnation for those who belong to Christ Jesus. And because you belong to him, the power of the life-giving Spirit has freed you from the power of sin that leads to death." The abundant life is a return to innocence and freedom from the spiritual weight of the sinful nature. Love and forgiveness rule in Christ, and guilt is a lie. We now have the opportunity to live with God through life in the Spirit (Romans 8:4).

In order for God's plan to be complete, Jesus had to leave, and the Holy Spirit came to teach and guide each of us. Just as Jesus was the disciples' personal connection to God, the Holy Spirit is our personal connection. As we learn to live life according to the Spirit, we become increasingly aware that God is with us personally. In this way, we live with God now, even before heaven is made manifest. Through life in the Spirit, we have a foretaste of eternal rewards that draw us to keep seeking God. Heaven is living with God for eternity, and it starts now! As we take hold of God's promises by believing His Word, we draw the supernatural into our everyday experience.

Jesus begins His famous Sermon on the Mount in Matthew chapter five by describing life in God's kingdom. He describes a happy, prosperous, and joy-filled life regardless of outward condition or circumstances, simply by resting humbly in God's salvation and favor. He describes a life completely satisfied by the revelation of God's matchless grace and salvation and how this causes a person to enjoy the earth and its blessings more than most. In this life, earthly riches become an unnecessary addition, a bonus to an already rich existence. Jesus describes a life beyond the scope of this world, which enables God's children to walk above pain and suffering.

However, all too often, our spiritual story identifies more with the Israelites than with Jesus. Like the Israelites of the Old Testament, we get distracted, confused, and discouraged by the difficulties in our life. We lose track of God and His purpose because our focus is down below instead of up above. We lack vision and become spiritually depressed. We forget that we have been saved *and* delivered. By default, we live out of our flesh.

When Jesus came to Earth, He showed us exactly how to live life with God, even while living in the temporary flesh. He was the perfect example and showed us the way to abundant life. The Bible says that Jesus had two natures—divine nature with its capacity to please God and human nature with its capacity to sin. Jesus yielded to God's way of doing things; in everything, He sought God's will. He did what God did, said what God said, and went where God went. He lived a life fully submitted to His Father. Not only did Jesus overcome the flesh by walking fully in His divine nature (Hebrews 4:15), but also when He died on the cross, he put to death the nature of man (Romans 8:3). When we believe God to forgive us for our sin, Jesus takes the burden of our sinful nature and hands us His righteous nature in exchange (2 Corinthians 5:21). We take on the very nature of God when we believe Him for salvation (2 Peter 1:4). Just as Jesus and God were one while Jesus was on earth, so we are one with Jesus. This is an eternal and abundant life or, in other words, new life in Christ (2 Corinthians 5:17). We *now* have Jesus's spiritual nature and can walk by God's side. Our life is just as extraordinary as Christ's when He walked the earth. When God looks at us, He sees His Son. He's looking at our new nature. This is great news!

Jesus says in John 3:3 (ESV), "Truly, truly, I say to you, unless one is born again he cannot see the kingdom of God." To be born again is a way of describing the spiritual exchange that occurs when we believe Jesus to save us from our sin. Our old (sin) nature dies, and our new (divine) nature is born. It is only when we continually turn from this godless tendency within and embrace the nature given to us in Christ that we experience authentic (not manufactured) patience, kindness, gentleness, and self-control. These fruits flow naturally when we believe God's perspective about our circumstances. Abundant life springs forth from walking in obedience and being controlled by the Holy Spirit. This is the mark of a true disciple (Romans 8:14). Truly, we have been born again when we believe Jesus for salvation. We now have His nature within and can please God and walk with Him even while on earth. He opens our eyes to see the reality of His kingdom on earth, which causes us to experience abundant life. Very commonly, however, Christians have not yet realized their new and eternal nature.

Our spirit is our innermost part that becomes alive to God when we believe in salvation though Christ. Our human spirit is inhabited by the Holy Spirit, and He renews a right spirit within us (Psalm 51:10). This is the part of our being that informs everything we think, feel, say, and do. Since God is Spirit, it is in our spirit where we experience connection and fellowship with Him. We live in God's kingdom, hear God's voice, and experience eternal life through our renewed spirit. When a believer fails to make contact with God through their regenerated spirit, he or she continues to live life in a natural way or, in other words, according to the flesh. The flesh is simply this—everything in a believer that opposes God's nature. Our flesh includes our thoughts, feelings, and desires that have not yielded to the influence of the Holy Spirit. The flesh includes our physical bodies. The Spirit seeks to restore our entire being back into perfect harmony.

It is the role of the Holy Spirit to reveal Christ's nature in us. As we yield to our faith, the Spirit is able to reveal our true identity or who God created us to be. We experience the fullness of Christ when we know who we are and what God created us to do in His kingdom. We overcome our flesh and live out of our new nature when we walk according to the Spirit. He teaches us how to do life God's way—the way He intended for us to operate. Our works, the things we do, become the complete handiwork of God—divinely prompted, dependent on Him, and in His strength. In this way, we become acutely aware of His presence in our lives. Our new nature and true identity become apparent as we submit everything in us to the Spirit, even our physical bodies. Life becomes enjoyable as the Holy Spirit reveals Christ's divine nature within!

The work of the Spirit is a transformation from the inside out. When our heart is right, it causes us to do and say right things. God is so much more concerned with our inner life than what is on the outside, for He knows when our heart is right, everything we do pleases Him. Man in his natural way attempts to clean up the outside in an effort to be right with God on the inside. We try in our own effort to do and say the right things, even think and feel the right way. Jesus condemned the hypocrisy of the Pharisees in Matthew 23:25–28, comparing them to whitewashed tombs, seemingly pure on the outside but full of impurities on the inside.

John 3:6 says that the flesh (our natural being apart from the influence of the Holy Spirit) begets flesh, and all of our efforts done in the flesh cannot please God. Only the Spirit can do the work. With Christ, we worship God in spirit and truth (John 4:24), meaning we worship God on the inside and the outside as a whole and united person. This means we worship Him in both the spiritual and physical realms. In this way, living the abundant life is an inside out, upside down way of living. In Christ, our natural inclinations are replaced by God's inclinations. This includes new thoughts, new feelings, and new desires that cause us to live life in a whole new way. Our life becomes an extraordinary life.

The Spirit opens our eyes and ears and awakens us to new realities. We become alive as the Lord stirs our senses to realize things of the spiritual realm. This is meant to enhance our life, giving us awareness of greater purpose and power. As we believe God's perspective communicated through the Bible and the Holy Spirit, we begin to experience life in a whole new way. Because we see, hear, sense, and recognize God's work on earth, following Him becomes natural. We see the enemy's work, recognize it as a distraction, and are no longer bound by his authority. We walk in the power and authority of Christ, causing us to rise above the fallen condition of the world. We begin to recognize God's supernatural involvement in our life and in this world.

Abundant life is characterized by the "in Him" statements scattered across the New Testament. This life promises answers to prayers, great works of God, healing, insight, and understanding. Jesus said in John 10:12 (NASB), "Truly, truly, I say to you, he who believes in Me, the works that I do, he will do also; and greater works than these he will do; because I go to the Father." The works Jesus is referring to are miracles, or great manifestations of God's power. All too often, because of fear of the unknown, we have explained away God's deeds on earth. We refuse to believe the reality of His work and instead explain it away by human reason or dismiss it completely from our mind. If we humble ourselves to accept that there is a greater power than ourselves, our life becomes a treasure hunt as we seek and know that God is with us in a very powerful way. Even the most mundane occurrence becomes an opportunity for us to sense God's divine intervention. What a glorious existence we have! Powerful gifts of the Spirit (Ephesians 4 and 1 Corinthians 12) are expressed as we simply walk in Christ by the power of the Spirit.

We have the opportunity to come into agreement with God. Our old self has been crucified, we are no longer bound by the sinful nature, and we now have abundant life available in Christ. We have an option, a new way of life that comes from the Holy Spirit's presence within. Our new reality is in God's kingdom filled with the power and authority of the Holy Spirit.

As Christians, our influence in the world comes from doing life in Christ by the empowerment of the Holy Spirit. Our lives become a living gospel. It is my passion and calling to see more people enjoying the life God offers in Christ. More than teaching what the Bible says about abundant life, I hope to illustrate the reality of it through my testimony. By sharing how the Spirit interacts with my daily life and circumstances, I hope to awaken desire within each of you to experience more in your relationship with Christ. To encourage you further, I have included a prayer at the end of each chapter and questions in the appendix for personal reflection. Grab some coffee and a journal and start interacting with God's Word in your own life and circumstances.

You may be wondering what abundant life looks like in everyday living. I'm an ordinary wife and mother living in the middle of a cornfield in Ohio. Through biblical and real-life examples, I hope to inspire you to hunger and thirst after God with all of your heart, soul, and strength. We simply cannot divorce ourselves from testimonies and stories in the Bible because our circumstances are different. We all have the common thread of the Spirit. My hope is that through sharing my experiences, you may be able to see your own life from a new perspective and realize your own abundant life available the moment you believe God's gift of salvation. And if you have not yet received this gift, don't wait! Whether you've heard it all your life, or you are hearing it for the first time, the gospel is a powerful message worthy of our careful attention and devotion. It is a message that gives more life every time we drink from its living waters.

"For God so loved the world, that he gave his only Son, that whoever believes in him should not perish but have eternal life" (John 3:16 ESV).

God sent Jesus to die for us. Jesus takes the burden of our sins and crucifies it on the cross. What do I mean by burden? All that judgment, shame, guilt, and ultimately death is gone! Not only did Jesus die on the cross and pay the price of our judgment, but also God raised Him from the grave, giving us His life. Jesus takes the spiritual weight of our sin and hands us His righteousness in exchange. We have new life empowered by the Holy Spirit to overcome the flesh and live in God's kingdom here and now. Let Him reveal this new reality in you today!

Dear Father, I desire for Your reality to be my reality. I humble myself to receive Your forgiveness and submit to Your Spirit. Even now, I feel the burden of sin lifting from my shoulders. Guide me into eternal life, allowing me to experience an abundant life on earth. Thank you for the extraordinary life you offer me in Christ. Teach me what this means in everyday living.

Chapter 2

Walking in Forgiveness

One day, I was recovering from doing something I knew to be wrong. I confessed to God but was caught somewhere between my sin and forgiveness. I could sense the Holy Spirit was grieved by my disobedience, and I was saddened by the seeming separation. Instead of wallowing over my sinfulness, which is so easy to do, I stepped into repentance. What this means is that I turned my mind from my old way of thinking in the flesh, about my sin, to think about that which pleases God. I focused all my energy on being led by the Spirit.

I pulled into a shopping center when an old man on the side of the road caught my attention. He was asking for help. I knew God was prompting me to give, so I prepared my offering as I was leaving the store. I positioned my minivan in front of the man and could sense there was something very different about this situation. He gradually rose from the camping chair where he was seated and steadily walked toward my van. Cars began to reroute as this encounter was already taking extra time.

When he reached my van, he was rambling about needing a watch. We exchanged a few words, and he asked if he could take my hand. I was surprised by how clean his hand felt. He kissed it and looked me straight in the eye. He delivered the most beautiful word of God that healed my heart in an instant. He said that if I asked God, He would clean my whole body. My eyes were drawn toward the silver cross hanging around his neck. I sincerely thanked him.

As I drove away, God's love enveloped me. I was grateful for His confirmation and encouraged to believe the truth about my sin and forgiveness. By the blood of Christ, I am clean. I'm honestly not sure if the old man was homeless or an angel. Either way, God used him to deeply touch my heart.

If we are to understand repentance in the context of our own life, it is helpful to understand from what we are turning and to what we should turn. When John the Baptist went into his preaching ministry, Matthew 3:2 says his message was, "Repent, for the kingdom of heaven is at hand!" John was sent to prepare the way for Jesus as Lord. We see the purpose of John's ministry as prophesied in Isaiah 40:3 (NKJV):

> The voice of one crying in the wilderness:
> "Prepare the way of the Lord;
> Make straight in the desert
> A highway for our God."

The same Spirit who motivated John the Baptist also prepares a pathway for Jesus to come as Lord of our life and to rule and shepherd us. The Spirit prepares our heart for the kingdom of heaven. God commands Isaiah to "Cry out!" and Isaiah wisely asks God, "What shall I cry?" God answers in verses 6–8:

> All flesh is grass,
> And all its loveliness is like the flower of
> the field.
> The grass withers, the flower fades,

> Because the breath of the Lord blows
> upon it;
> Surely the people are grass.
> The grass withers, the flower fades,
> But the word of our God stands forever.

All flesh is temporary; it is earthbound and passes away with the earth. The great news is God breathes upon our flesh through the Holy Spirit who speaks God's word into our very life. We stand with God forever. If we are to experience eternal life, we must turn from all that is temporary within to the life given to us by Christ's resurrection. This is why Paul writes in 1 Corinthians 15:31 (KJV), "I die daily." Daily, he identifies that which is not from God and leans into the life-giving Spirit in order to experience spiritual resurrection in the kingdom of heaven even before bodily resurrection.

The truth is we are regenerated the moment we believe and are instantly a new creation (2 Corinthians 5:17). This is eternal truth. However, we live in the temporal, in the flesh, which is bound by time. In our experience, it seems as though we still have our sin nature, and there is a struggle between our flesh and our renewed spirit. One moment we are walking in righteousness, and the next we are lowered to the natural response of human nature. Paul expresses this struggle in Romans 7. In verse 14 (NLT), he writes, "So the trouble is not with the law, for it is spiritual and good. The trouble is with me, for I am all too human, a slave to sin." He continues to communicate how it feels like his old and new nature are at war, desiring to do God's will but failing to reach the standard. Here's the great news: "And because you belong to him, the power of the life-giving Spirit has freed you from the power of sin that leads to death." (Romans 8:2 NLT)

Christ died to free us from the power of the sinful nature; we are no longer dictated by its cravings. In Him, we have another option. Instead of trying, failing, trying again, and failing again, there is a new way for those who are in Christ. We set our mind on the things above, directing all our faculties toward God. We are focused on the Holy Spirit who is teaching us to walk in a new way, the way God intended when He created each of us. We live a new life controlled by the Holy Spirit. Not only does He prompt us, but also He empowers us. His presence is a habitation, not just visitation.

From our perspective, transformation feels like a process, but from God's perspective, it is (already) complete. He is looking at us from an eternal perspective through the blood of Christ. We have an opportunity to come into agreement with God and live like His promises are true. When our eyes are focused on who we are in Christ, that is who we become. In this way, the struggle with the flesh naturally becomes less and less. In order to experience this transformation, it is essential we quit focusing on our sins. It is essential that when we realize that we have fallen short, we turn and fully receive God's forgiveness.

How do we know what is temporary unless God reveals it? We must allow the Spirit to search our heart and search our soul. As we consume truth, as we allow His word to penetrate our heart, as we realize more of God's character revealed *in us*—all that opposes becomes clear. When we read the Bible, the Holy Spirit reveals God's heart. The Spirit's testimony within our spirit will tell us when we have transgressed. We must step quickly into repentance when the Holy Spirit convicts, lest our flesh and the enemy rise to condemn. There is no need for a Christian to remain in feelings of guilt.

God's forgiveness is tangible. It's not some far away dream we know to be true, but experience the contrary while we are here. It is not intended that we exist in a lake of regret and condemnation for what we did or did not do. The new reality is that we have freedom in Christ. Today, when we step into obedience to the Holy Spirit, God is able to confirm us in our everyday life, as He did to me through the man on the side of the road. When God is able to interact with us on such a personal level, we are consumed by love and forgiveness, so that when our flesh rises or the enemy attacks, we dismiss the lies and remain unharmed in our soul. Our heart remains free. The enemy's lies, often projected on to us by other people through guilt and shame, only harm us when we believe them. People's words cause us to stumble when we allow lies to replace God's truth in our heart.

We have an opportunity in Christ to take our shame, our guilt, and condemnation to the throne of God and receive forgiveness. In the world, we will be told that we are at fault, and we will feel the burden of responsibility on our shoulders. But in Christ, there is a different way. We have the opportunity to go to God, lay our burdens down, and listen to the truth. Sometimes, we will hear God correcting us and showing us a new way. When God corrects, we do not feel condemned but relieved; His way is like a breath of fresh air. And sometimes the worldly guilt and blame will be unjust. Either way, we walk forward in forgiveness. We let go of our failures, walk in newness of life, and are naturally able to extend forgiveness to our accusers because we no longer feel the burden of accusation.

There was a situation in a reputable organization where my oldest son, DJ, was being held accountable for someone else's mistake. He was a student leader, and someone in his group failed to fulfill his commitment. DJ didn't understand why he was responsible for something he could not control. My sensitive son felt he was being blamed, and it devastated him. The burden of responsibility was weighing on DJ's spirit.

The issue at hand was that DJ had internalized blame, and it was at war with God's truth inside of him. The Lord instructed me to tell DJ the good news—that the whole reason Jesus came and died on the cross was to remove the judgment he was feeling. I encouraged him to take the weight and set it down at the foot of the throne. As soon as I spoke this good news to my son, he was delivered and his spirit lifted.

The advice given to young Martin Luther has proven helpful in my own life. When Luther struggled deeply with the spiritual weight of his sin, Dr. Johann von Staupitz advised him to pray through Psalm 119:94. When the pang of regret stings, when guilt creeps in, when I remember my faults, like Luther, I pray, "Lord, please save me. I am Yours."

It is helpful to understand the way God treats us as His children. Because of the way we have been treated in the world, it is natural to believe God handles us in the same way. Sometimes, it is difficult for us to realize and grasp His forgiveness. He is more patient with our immaturities than we may believe. One day, my boys were fighting. DJ was clearly frustrated by his younger brother, Isaac. They were playing outside, and Isaac kept messing up DJ's plans to make a fort, so the mutual annoyance began. In that moment, I decided it was time to show them another way. I gathered the boys, and we talked about how God treats us when we "mess up" His plan. We decided He forgives, accepts, and teaches. I asked them to think about how they were treating each other and how that worked out for them. We decided to press the "redo" button and try it again with a new perspective. An hour later, both boys were beaming. They experienced God's joy, peace, and contentment as a result of doing it His way.

The greatest need of the human heart is forgiveness. Walking in forgiveness is necessary in order to have consistent fellowship with God and others. Without it, we cannot enjoy the deep, intimate connection that God desires. We become angry and bitter toward others and, ultimately, toward God.

When we refuse to forgive, when we allow our feelings to stew to the point where we can no longer be around that person or look them in the eye, this behavior can be an indication that we have not yet fully received God's forgiveness. Forgiveness is a free gift, and we cannot freely give to others what we have not first received. The pride that causes us to refuse to forgive also blinds us to the hardness of our own heart. Our willingness to forgive those who have offended or hurt us is directly connected to our own forgiveness. Bitterness is a dangerous place to stay.

Unforgiveness is a disease of the heart. Sometimes we say the words, "I forgive you," but our heart is far from forgiveness because the pain is just too real. Forgiveness is not denial of emotion. By definition, of course, we don't know when we are in denial! Denial is a very natural response to pain; it is a survival technique of the flesh. Instead of running to God, pouring out our feelings, and allowing Him to heal the disease, we simply ignore or refuse to allow ourselves to feel a certain way. This is not only incredibly unhealthy for our emotional well-being but also very harmful to our spiritual life. Unhealed pain in the heart becomes darkened corners, darkened corners become hardness, and hardened areas of the heart are hostile to God and His Spirit. When our feelings are hurt, it is comforting to know Jesus experienced similar emotions. Realizing Jesus knows how we feel may be all that is needed to let it go.

We must understand it is our pride that causes us to become offended, and we choose whether or not we are upset by other people. One day, I was working at our church to prepare our new building for services. I had been given a task by another volunteer and happily worked on my assignment. Suddenly, the overseer appeared and was upset that I was working on that particular project. I could see that she was very stressed, and without inspecting my work, she told me to stop and kicked me out of the area. I was at a loss. I tried to start another task, but feeling deflated, I eventually left. On my way home, I told the Lord that I felt like crap. He said, "My Son knows how you feel." This gentle reminder was all I needed to forgive and move on.

In high school, I had the wonderful opportunity to work closely with our youth pastor as a student leader. My male counterpart, John, was a friend I dearly loved and admired. He was incredibly talented and a strong leader. Not only were we part of the planning and organization of our youth group, but also we were personally discipled by our pastor and met on a regular basis to discuss reading assignments, and life in general. This was a phenomenal opportunity to grow into the leaders God created us to be.

John and I went our separate ways in college. John was so talented that he majored in English and continued on to medical school after graduation. As I was starting my family, John was in his residency. In 2006, my young family and I were in my hometown visiting my parents. A flood of phone calls streamed into my parents' house with rumors that John had committed suicide. Immediately, I rejected the idea and denied my grief; my emotions were channeled into anger.

Indeed, suicide was just a rumor. John had died from an anaphylactic reaction to a substance used to cut cocaine. He was a secret addict who struggled to overcome his addiction all throughout college. Having already returned home to Cincinnati, I decided not to travel back for the funeral. I spoke to our youth pastor and thought that I would be fine. I wrote John an angry letter and filed it away thinking I had put it all to rest. Little did I know there was a sickness growing inside; I was carrying a seed of bitterness. From time to time, I would return to the angry letter and stew over the shame of it all. I would look at the funeral notice and think about what might have been. I didn't realize I was refusing to forgive John. I should have known something was wrong when I was surprised and slightly annoyed by classmates' questions at our high school reunion the year after his death.

Just before Easter of 2008, God started to work on my heart. He led me to a website John's parents had created. It was an organization and scholarship program designed to help other parents and children struggling with drug addiction. When I explored the impact John was having on so many people, my heart began to soften. God has been accomplishing all He had in mind through John's life and death.

On Easter Sunday, our church had a call to repentance. When unforgiveness was mentioned, God pierced my heart. "I've forgiven John," He said, "Have you?" Tears flowed freely down my face as I confessed my unbelief and lack of forgiveness. For the first time, I honestly mourned my great friend.

Lord, I open my heart to You. Search me and know me. Continue to open my eyes to what you see. Deal with my sin, leading me into sweet repentance. Reveal any unforgiveness I have unknowingly stored in my heart and heal my wounds. Shed light on the darkened areas and massage my hardened heart. Give me a tender, obedient heart that is responsive to Your Spirit.

Chapter 3

Faith like a Child

We knew Lucy, a gorgeous blue Weimaraner, since she was born. Fearsome and strong, she made herself known to all who could hear. She was born to love. She loved having fun, loved people, and loved attention. We brought her home when she was six weeks old, and she cried all the way. She whined the whole night and any moment she was not in our arms. She had a will stronger than any. We battled her day and night, trying our best to raise her with discipline and love. She had too much energy, so we ran her long and hard. In her second year, she was my training partner for a marathon. I needed her just as much as she needed the exercise.

Despite our best efforts, something wasn't quite right; she was anxious and hyperactive. Not only would she bark incessantly, but also, she would panic whenever I left. She was so excitable that she'd forget her manners and accidentally hurt people. She was discontent. *Where have we gone wrong? Have we failed?* The decision was reached that we could do no more, and she needed to go somewhere she could be challenged, where she could excel and shine.

Before we go any further, let us consider the origin of our faith. What is faith? Is it something we use our mind to believe? Is it something we do? Is it conviction or trust? The answer is yes, but we must first consider the origin. Belief does not cause faith. Action does not cause faith. Trust does not cause faith. The origin of our faith in Christ is God; it is of God. Ephesians 2:8–9 (NASB) says, "For by grace you have been saved through faith; and that not of yourselves, it is the gift of God." The Bible is clear that the entire salvation experience is not of our own doing. Belief, action, and trust are therefore a reaction to the faith God puts in our heart. Unless the Spirit influences and opens our mind to faith, we cannot believe. Let's consider what the writer of Hebrews has to say about faith, because the words in chapter eleven are incredible! Hebrews 11:1 (AMP) says:

> Now faith is the assurance (the confirmation, the title deed) of the things [we] hope for, being the proof of things [we] do not see and the conviction of their reality [faith perceiving as real fact what is not revealed to the senses].

Human beings have an amazing capacity to believe. Our beliefs shape our perceptions that inform our interactions with this world. Our beliefs come from thoughts and feelings based on information and experience; therefore, as we gather more information or have more experiences, our beliefs change. Faith that is of God never changes.

Many believe a certain government system is better than others. Many believe vitamins, diet, and exercise will make you healthier. Many believe a certain lifestyle is better than others. As humans, we put our trust in these things. But then something happens. A government fails. The person who exercises and takes vitamins gets cancer. The person with a better lifestyle dies young anyway. This is what happens when we put our trust in something of this world—our beliefs shift with the wind. We can see this shifting of worldly wisdom as the advice from experts changes with every generation. It is a case of misplaced trust.

Faith becomes reality as we reach into the unseen world, grasp God's promises, and draw them into this world. It is the basis of our perspective and the way we see this life. It's not just something we do on Sundays, something we study, or something we blindly follow. It is our entire existence, our being at our very core. It is our work, our play, our home life, and our public life.

Faith is to perceive things as they truly are. The human heart is proficient at denial, but God opens our soul to light. The Gospel invites us to live in the real reality, even if our natural senses cannot perceive it at first. God opens our eyes and our ears; and we taste, feel, and smell His goodness. He heightens our spiritual senses, and we attain His promises by faith. Faith becomes tangible as we live out those promises in our everyday life.

By the Holy Spirit, faith seeks to influence our entire being. What starts in our inner spirit works outward, influencing our thoughts, emotions, and desires before spilling out into reality by our actions. Faith seeks to inform our thinking, which changes our feelings, which together remake our desires; we naturally act out God's will.

Faith is of the spirit (1 Corinthians 12:9), and belief is of the mind. Faith necessarily influences beliefs, but sometimes our mind gets in the way. God puts faith in our spirit, yet our mind may create a barrier so we cannot see the proof of our faith! We know we have faith, but we have a hard time believing, so we never experience confirmation of our faith on this earth. Our heart fails when we cannot see or sense God is pleased with us.

God so lovingly wants to give us proof of our salvation and new life. There is so, so much more to life than fleeting good times. There's a depth, a richness, a layer of eternity that God wants to add. He desires to enhance our existence so that we actually receive a bit of our heavenly inheritance here on earth. We experience God's promises by being sustained and controlled by faith. We trust naturally because we have experience and tangible confirmation through the Holy Spirit. What we do, say, and feel become the proof of our faith.

"Truly I tell you," Jesus said in Matthew 18:3 (NIV), "unless you change and become like little children, you will never enter the kingdom of heaven." Again, in Luke 18:16 (NIV), Jesus drew a child to His side and said, "Let the little children come to me, and do not hinder them, for the kingdom of God belongs to such as these."

As I contemplate the faith Jesus is commending in these verses, I look to the children in my own life. I have been given the opportunity to teach a large group of children, K-4th grade, at our church. The first thing I noticed is that I don't have to prove the Word to them. When I teach, they receive the message without hindrance. Children are open and teachable; their hearts are soft and moldable. Their faith is pure and uncomplicated, and there is little resistance to the Gospel. They have a natural humility that allows them to innocently accept God's Word. While a child may not be perfect in obedience, a child can be redirected and taught the correct way. A child is quick to forgive and quick to give up offenses. They do not carry the burdens of the world, the weight that comes with responsibility.

The faith of a child is willing. We look to Mary, mother of Jesus, as an example of a willing heart. An angel, Gabriel, delivered unbelievable news that Mary was to give birth to the Son of God in Luke 1:31. Even though it was impossible since she was a virgin, Mary chose to believe God. We see Mary's submission in verse 36 (NIV) when she said, "I am the Lord's servant. May your word to me be fulfilled." Having no regard for her own desires, she submitted to the Lord's plan and innocently trusted God's will.

Not long ago, I noticed our church was having a baptism service for children. I asked Isaac, my eight-year-old, if he would like to be baptized.

"Yeah, I want to be baptized!" he exclaimed.

My heart smiled, not only because my child desired to be obedient but also because of his faith. He didn't ask questions or need more information. His conscience told him baptism was a good thing, and he was willing!

After realizing we needed to find our dog Lucy a new home, the last two weeks were very difficult for me. I was sad about having to say goodbye. We changed her rules and put even more boundaries in place. Things were peaceful, but could she keep it up? Was there any possible way she could stay with our family and everyone could be happy? As I had done continuously through the two years of her life, I prayed. I prayed she could stay; I prayed she could change; I prayed we could change. But most importantly, I prayed His will be done. I was all out of ideas, but one thing was clear—God was telling me I needed to be willing to give up Lucy. I was reminded of Abraham and Isaac and realized my sacrifice was not nearly as difficult.

But what happens when we don't have a willing heart? At some point, our will is going to conflict with the will of God. Our mind will reason, our emotions might flare, and we must look to Jesus in these moments. We have a High Priest who has experience in the flesh and understands our weakness (Hebrews 4:15). The night Jesus was arrested, he went to the Garden of Gethsemane to prepare himself. Of course, he didn't want to be beaten and die on a cross! He was filled with such great anxiety, and I have heard some people say that they believe He actually sweat blood as indicated by Luke's account (Luke 22:44). What Jesus said in Matthew 26:41 (NIV) was profound, "The spirit is willing, but the flesh is weak." His mind was reeling, His emotions were screaming, and He didn't want to go through the agony of the cross. It wasn't the physical pain He agonized over, it was the looming separation from His Father as He took the weight of sin. Even still, in Luke 22:42 (NIV), Jesus said, "Yet not My will, but Yours be done."

Recently, my duty as a storyteller to the children in our church included acting and singing. The writers of the curriculum decided it would be a good idea to sing half the lesson so they rewrote the lyrics of eight popular songs. While I thought it sounded like a lot of fun, I immediately recognized the difficulty of the task. I asked the worship leader if she would be willing to sing the songs, but she declined. I asked two other musically capable people, but they were unable to help either. By Wednesday morning at Women's Bible Study, I was discouraged.

While the Bible teacher spoke, I heard the Lord say, "I want you to sing the message." Within two minutes, the teacher said, "I am the Lord, I have a voice, and I am using it to sing over you." I sat at attention and wrote down what the Lord was clearly saying to me. Later, I shared the message with my small group. "But," I confessed, "I don't have the 'chops' to sing those songs." My sweet friend looked me in the eye and said, "Lisa, if the Lord is calling you to do this, then He will supernaturally gift you to accomplish the task."

I knew she spoke truth and went home to put in the hours of preparation. As I practiced, the Lord began releasing the notes in my voice. My improvement was amazing, not perfect, but amazing. However, I still had to execute the task despite my great fear. I attended church service before

I needed to present the musical to the children and was encouraged. The pastor's wife was speaking that day, and she admitted that at first, she didn't want to give the sermon. I watched as the Lord blessed her obedience. All the worship songs were about overcoming fear, and I allowed God's truth to calm my nerves. I performed the story and was told that the children were touched. The Lord had accomplished His will through me despite my fear and lack of ability.

A child's faith is innocent with freedom to obey God uninhibited. Innocence from a spiritual perspective is liberty from the burden of sin. When we trust Jesus, we return to the innocence of a child. If we are to understand the type of relationship God intends to have with His creation, we must look to the garden before the Fall. When God created Adam and Eve, everything they had came from God. They walked with God and communicated with Him completely uninhibited. Perfection consisted of a relationship free from distraction, barriers, or fear. God gave them responsibility, dominion, and authority over all other creation, yet there was no power struggle. They knew Who created them and knew Who made them capable. Living within God's established orderliness, they felt no burden for the task at hand. They lived abundantly. This is the relationship God desires to restore in each of us.

Unfortunately, it is not long before we are touched by evil, and experience teaches us not to trust; consequently, we are naturally suspicious of God. Fear drives us to control and innocence erodes as maturity necessitates responsibility. Our own desires are born and preferences develop. We take on the burdens of this world and increasingly become independent of God. When in truth, independence in this world comes through dependence on God, not on our own ability to meet expectations. Just as a child is dependent on their parent to provide, so we are dependent on God. Often, this is the missing link in our life. It is not our own means through which we trust for our daily provision, but on God. While we can believe this truth in our mind, the way we live our life and the burdens we carry may suggest otherwise. In some ways, the poor and destitute are better off than the rich and powerful. Just as Jesus warned in Matthew 19:24, it is much harder for the rich person to depend on and trust God because there is no personal need. The same is true with people who are beautiful, talented, and intelligent. We become competent in our own ability and create an illusion of control and become self-reliant.

Fullness in Christ cannot be experienced without innocence and maturity. The world presents these two concepts as mutually exclusive, but in Christ, we have both. We are adopted into the kingdom as a child of God, and we take on the innocent faith of a child as we trust Him. We become independent of this world and our old nature and become dependent on Him in our new nature. With humble, unpretentious faith, we rely on God to provide. He gives us the ability to live without selfish ambition, pride, or haughtiness. We innocently follow Him and trust Him to take care of us, just as a child follows and trusts his parent.

Living hand in hand with Christ, we are enabled to live our entire lives pleasing to God. We walk with God, and He teaches us how to do life with Him. He restores our innocence, meaning we become like a child in our spirit, yet are maturing as a result. He protects us from the spiritual weight of sin and evil in and around us. He frees us from the daily burdens of life to serve Him. Our minds are clear to focus on the eternal. These thoughts bring us joy, peace, and gladness.

A child's faith is pure. In the Bible, David gives us an intimate view of a man after God's own heart. When David was a child, he was a lowly shepherd. He was an innocent boy, blessed by God in all that he did simply by trusting and following Him. He spent years and years leaning into God's character. God taught him how to shepherd, and from that, David understood his relationship to Him. When David wrote, "The Lord is my shepherd; I shall not want" (Psalm 23:1 ESV), he wrote it from his experience with God. He hung out with God and got to know Him as a friend. He took his fear to Him and listened for His answer. He let God inform him about his life and circumstances. David's heart became like God's heart as he followed Him through the bends and turns, ups and downs, of life.

God taught David about Himself through the role of a shepherd. The job of a shepherd is to lead, protect, and care for his sheep. David intimately knew the dependence of a sheep upon the shepherd for survival. Through this understanding, he knew God as his Lord. He recognized that without God, he was lost, was easily led astray, and could not survive alone. He sought Him for guidance, direction, and comfort. David knew God as Provider of all his needs and was satisfied in Him. In those fields, tending to his sheep, he learned what it meant to totally depend on God.

Despite the abuses he experienced and the injustice of his situation, David remained pure in heart. He became a gifted musician, mighty warrior, and anointed King of Israel. The current King Saul was so jealous, he wanted David dead. One of the things I love about the Psalms is the way David expresses so many emotions and how God speaks to and changes those emotions when David comes to Him. There are multiple Psalms where David pours out his natural, human feelings about his circumstances. David also writes magnificent Psalms elevating God as Supreme Power. God takes his fear, disappointment, and anger and teaches David to see from His perspective. The natural response is deep-felt, genuine praise, and adoration. God personally touches

David's heart and heals the offense. As a result, David's heart remains soft, alive, and responsive to the Holy Spirit.

The challenge is to remain pure in heart despite the enemy's influence. When I was young, I played several instruments, including the piano. I learned music in a traditional setting, and the structure of written music provided a wonderful learning environment. I bounced effortlessly along, not too concerned about mistakes made. When I graduated from high school, the music stopped. I didn't study music in college and was distracted with other things. After college, I got married, and we started our family. Eventually, I inherited my grandmother's baby grand piano and returned to making music, but the music didn't flow. I was bogged down by all the rules, bound by the notes written on the page. Consumed standards and expectations created a barrier. Instead of enjoying the journey to perfection, my pride informed me I had to be perfect now. Fear crippled and inhibited my ability to be used by God in this area of my life. I realized that in order to be a usable vessel, I needed to transition into a contemporary style of music, including learning to play by chords. One night, I sat down at Barnes and Noble with a music book and allowed the Holy Spirit to teach me a new way of making music. I had to let go of the rules of tradition in order to operate freely in the realm of music.

Sheet music had been like the sheepfold Jesus talks about in John 10. If you are unfamiliar with this parable, please pause to read John 10:1–22. In order to understand what Jesus was communicating through the story of the Good Shepherd, we must recognize it as an illustration of what was happening at the end of John 9. Verses 40–41 (NIV) say, "Some Pharisees who were with him heard him say this and asked, 'What? Are we blind too?' Jesus said, 'If you were blind, you would not be guilty of sin; but now that you claim you can see, your guilt remains.'" In chapter 10,

Jesus sets up the parable of the sheepfold, the door, and the shepherd. Jesus accused the Pharisees of being a thief who does not enter by the door, but climbs up some other way. God's Law of the Old Testament created the standards of the sheepfold that kept God's chosen people safe while they waited for the time to come out. Jesus was the door—His salvation making it possible to enter the sheepfold. Those who believed God for salvation entered through the door, even before salvation was made manifest through Jesus. The Pharisees had climbed up over the standards of God's Law to enter the sheepfold. They did not know or recognize Jesus because they had not entered through His salvation. After accusing the Pharisees of being a thief, Jesus hits them hard with this statement in John 10:10 (ESV): "The thief comes only to steal and kill and destroy. I came that they may have life and have it abundantly."

In my early adult life, I found myself safe within the sheepfold of the church. However, I was listening to and distracted by the enemy's lies. My faith became tainted. The rules and confines of false religion were creating a barrier so His Spirit couldn't flow. God was calling me to follow Him into an intimate relationship with Himself. In John 10:11, Jesus identifies Himself as the Good Shepherd who lays down His life for the sheep and leads them into rich pastures. The true sheep follow Him because they know His voice. Jesus was calling my name, and it was time for me to follow Him out of the sheepfold. Letting go of the rules and standards of man's tradition was part of learning to be led by the Holy Spirit into abundant life.

Our negative experiences in life can challenge the purity of our faith. If we are to trust God as our Lord, we must believe and not doubt His providence despite our difficulties in this present age. Nothing comes to us but what is filtered through His hand. God is good all the time and is for us, not against.

When we are faithful, we view life through the perspective of our faith. We must allow Him to open our eyes to see His guidance, help, and council, even in tragic circumstances.

I enjoyed our last days with Lucy more than ever. I took pictures of her, we had fun, and I treasured our happy moments together. We swam, we fished, and we walked. I watched her bounce in the tall grass, dashing up the hill to get a drink of water in the pond, and then come barreling down. Boy, did I love her. One night after dinner was cleaned up and the children were settled down for stories, I took her out for an evening walk. She had been in all day, so I kept her off the leash. We were a quarter a mile away, but suddenly, she saw the dog across the road and started running. I called her and realized there was a car coming around the bend. She paused in the ditch and I thought she'd stop. The neighbor was calling her dog, unknowingly named Lucy also. At the last second, my Lucy dashed into the road. The driver never saw her before impact and just kept going.

I screamed. A group of neighbors came to help. I was in a daze and let the others arrange everything; I just did what I was told. I cradled her head as she struggled to catch her breath. Lucy lifted her head and looked long and hard into my eyes. I knew what needed to be done as we nuzzled our noses. Lucy knew she was loved, and I knew she loved me. I enjoyed the moment and cherished her like never before.

In the days following the accident, I struggled to understand why God would allow such a horrible thing to happen. As I grieved the loss of our dog, I realized what seemed to be irony was actually God's divine purpose. He beautifully orchestrated the sequence of events that unfolded, and I marveled at His wisdom and insight. He allowed the accident to happen, but not before preparing me for her death. I cherished those end days with Lucy not knowing they were her last. I was overwhelmed by God's love and care for his sheep.

When we allow faith to flood our perspective, God helps us through the difficult events that are inevitable in this fallen world, and our faith remains pure. He binds our broken heart and heals it, bringing us to a place of wholeness. When we accept God's perspective, letting go of our own, we rise above the heartbreak and avoid the many pitfalls common to the human heart. Through faith, we are saved. These devastating events need not dictate the rest of our experience on earth. By allowing God access into our pain, He brings beauty from the ashes. After such a traumatic event, we thought we would never have another dog. However, in time, God brought a precious shih tzu poodle to our home. Chester has been an absolute delight and true blessing to our family, a constant reminder of God's compassion and care.

In the Bible, both David and Mary asked God questions when they didn't understand. Mary asked how she would become pregnant. Because Mary asked in faith and not doubt, the angel was able to explain how it would happen. David often asked God why and how long He would allow his troubling circumstances to continue. Because David poured out his heart, God poured His perspective into David. Instead of doubting or accusing God, David went to Him for comfort, council, and guidance. Despite temptation and natural desires, David did life God's way. He was enabled to do this because he allowed God's thoughts, feelings, and desires to replace his own. When we believe Jesus, He takes those burdens that weigh heavy on our heart and gives us rest. We become like a child in faith—willing, innocent, and pure.

Dear precious Jesus, place in me an open, willing heart, and teachable spirit. Take me back to innocence, revealing the lies that are stealing the abundant life You died to give me. Purify my faith. Open my eyes and ears to spiritual realities, so I may learn to follow You as a child follows a parent.

Chapter 4

Wilderness Experience

In the opening chapter, I described an abundant life. This is a rich and full life filled with purpose and satisfaction. This life produces spiritual fruit like love, joy, peace, patience, and self-control. This life is marked by supernatural gifts and works of the Spirit. It is the life God promises, yet Christians often find themselves in the space between a promise and its fulfillment. This space between can be described as a wilderness experience.

It is God who saved the Israelites from the oppression of slavery and God who delivered them out of Egypt. It is also God who led them into the wilderness, the desert between Egypt and the Promised Land. It is in the wilderness where God tested their faith.

Jesus also was led into the wilderness, as well as Abraham, David, John the Baptist, and many other heroes of the faith. In fact, it is a normal experience for God to lead His people into the wilderness. Leading us through the wilderness is an act of divine love and grace. It is in the wilderness where God trains us into realizing unbroken fellowship with Him.

Because we are in the state of being redeemed but not yet glorified, it may seem as though our fellowship is broken as we make our way in life. But in truth, this is not the case, for God's Spirit resides in us. It is in the wilderness where God purifies our beliefs and where He deals with our sin, so we can walk victoriously above the flesh. It is in the wilderness where He teaches us to obey so that we may know without a shadow of doubt that He is continually with us. The wilderness is where God proves our faith to us.

The definition of prove is to demonstrate the truth or existence of (something) by evidence or argument. We may be inclined to believe that we prove our faith to God, but what is actually happening is that God is proving our faith to us. Faith is a gift (1 Corinthians 12:9) God places in our spirit. When we struggle, we have an opportunity to let our faith rise into action; and in this way, God proves faith exists in us. Faith becomes reality as it is expressed in this world. Faith becomes our light in the darkness of the wilderness.

It may seem as though God is distant in the wilderness, but indeed, we learn from the Israelites that God is ever present, providing, protecting, and leading. During their time in the desert, God miraculously provided food and water. Deuteronomy 29:5 states that He provided clothes and shoes the entire forty years they wandered. Exodus 13:21–22 explains how God gave them a pillar of cloud by day to lead them and a pillar of fire by night to give them light.

God's presence was undeniable, yet the Israelites never experienced Him quite like Moses did. They complained. They lost hope. They despaired. When things got tough, they went back to their old way of life. They did what they thought was right instead of obeying God's expressed commands. Disobedience extinguishes our awareness of God's presence; we break connection with God's Spirit and feel lost. Most of the Israelites died in the wilderness, never experiencing God's promise. There is a close link between disobedience and unbelief. It is written in Hebrews 3:18–19 (NIV), "And to whom did God swear that they would never enter his rest if not to those who disobeyed? So we see that they were not able to enter, because of their unbelief."

Jesus's experience in the wilderness was very difficult as well. According to the Gospel of Matthew, right after He was baptized and the Holy Spirit came and remained with Him, God sent Jesus into the wilderness where He was tested and tried. His physical body was brought to nothing as He did not eat or drink for forty days. Satan came and tempted Him, attacking Jesus at His very core. Jesus focused. He allowed the experience to destroy His flesh. The testing served to prove Him and empower Him to complete God's purpose for His life. His experience qualified Him and made Him ready to complete God's ministry and purpose here on earth. He responded to the test in the way God would have Him respond, and He was released victoriously.

Graduation from high school was the moment of truth in my spiritual life. I knew God well enough at the time to understand He had called me and had a plan for my life. Like any child in faith, I didn't know exactly what that looked like, but I had an inkling He was calling me into His service. God had given me an intelligent mind, one that worked logically. I loved math and science, so engineering seemed like the right fit for me. I chose Purdue University with a major in engineering to prepare for life as an adult.

Immediately, I began to struggle in a way I had never experienced before. Homesickness hit hard, and school was crushingly difficult. I set my mind to my way and met the challenge of engineering with hard work and determination. I heard the statistics of engineer dropouts, especially among women, and took on the attitude of "Oh yeah, I'll show you!" As time progressed, I simply ignored the feeling that a part of me was dying.

Had I remained soft to God's gentle correction and my true feelings, there would have been no harm done to my spiritual health. Had I gone to Him with my struggles like David and surrendered my personal plan, He may have used engineering to guide me into His will. Or perhaps He would have prompted me to declare a new major. But I plodded forward in my own strength. My heart was shriveling and my spiritual life suffocating.

When we walk cross-grained to the will of God, our heart becomes hardened and calloused; we take on burdens we were never meant to carry. In our spirit, we are bent over, eyes to the ground, oblivious to the God of the universe who stretches out His hand to carry those burdens. Our spiritual eyesight is darkened and our hearing distorted; we do not see or hear God clearly.

A shroud of darkness covered me as I chose to live life independently of God's Spirit. Confusion, doubt, and fear gained entrance and threatened God's love and peace in my heart. My path became unclear, and I began to wonder where God was and what He was doing. Fortunately for me, my physical health deteriorated before my heart completely hardened to God's way for me. Two and a half years later, my body gave out and completely stopped me. I melted down and my parents came in the middle of the night to take me home. I was back to square one.

I scrambled to make it right. I switched my major and graduated from the University of Cincinnati with a BA in Spanish. The Lord guided me to marry a wonderful man named Casey, and we started our family. The Lord was always good and continually present, but I was lost in a spiritual wilderness. My focus was down below on the daily struggle, and I lost awareness of His presence. Satan found his foothold, and fear strengthened its grip on me. Loneliness set in, and anxiety rose.

I did not realize I was cultivating and practicing an unhealthy habit named worry. My thoughts always revolved around my brain since I was a little girl and that was normal for me. I would read Matthew 6:25 and think, "I have food; I have clothes; I'm good!" Plus, I have a bright and bubbly personality, so surely I was the least likely to struggle with my thoughts and emotions. However, any unrenewed mind is susceptible to the way of the world—a way filled with anxiety, stress, and overburden. By the time I had children, I felt as though a weight like a cat was lying on my chest. In my mid-twenties, I realized I was struggling with general anxiety.

My natural way was that of fear and anxiety, but in the wilderness, the Lord drew me out of the world and wooed me back into loving relationship with Himself. I knew anxiety wasn't from Him, but the result of sin in my flesh. I recognized a life filled with fear wasn't God's intention for me. I chose to believe God is good and desires good things for me. I chose to believe He was allowing me to struggle for my good, and the struggle was there for a purpose.

Hebrews 12:4–11 says that God is treating us as His children, and as His children, He disciplines us. Let's read this passage from The Message version:

> In this all-out match against sin, others have suffered far worse than you, to say nothing of what Jesus went through—all that bloodshed! So don't feel sorry for yourselves. Or have you forgotten how good parents treat children, and that God regards you as his children?
>
> My dear child, don't shrug
> off God's discipline,
> but don't be crushed by it either.

It's the child he loves that he disciplines;
the child he embraces, he also corrects.

God is educating you; that's why you must never drop out. He's treating you as dear children. This trouble you're in isn't punishment; it's training, the normal experience of children. Only irresponsible parents leave children to fend for themselves. Would you prefer an irresponsible God? We respect our own parents for training and not spoiling us, so why not embrace God's training so we can truly live? While we were children, our parents did what seemed best to them. But God is doing what is best for us, training us to live God's holy best. At the time, discipline isn't much fun. It always feels like it's going against the grain. Later, of course, it pays off handsomely, for it's the well-trained who find themselves mature in their relationship with God.

For ten years, I prayed that the Lord would take away my anxiety, and for ten years, I chose to believe He was allowing my condition to continue in order to train me. Like so many Biblical characters, God led our family into a physical wilderness. We moved to a house on fourteen wooded acres. The house was a half mile off the main road, and we were completely separated by trees. God had purposely set us apart and was sanctifying us for His use.

Anyone who struggles with difficulties such as anxiety, depression, or any other emotional disturbance readily admits there is a physical component to the struggle. I asked my doctor, and he suggested medication; however, I was nursing my son and didn't want to go down that road. I knew I could also address the issue through vigorous exercise. I had always wanted to run a marathon, so I took the opportunity to train.

Admittedly, I was a bit obsessed. Training for a marathon is intense, so I used my anxiety to focus and discipline me. The demand of running also caused me to become more aware of the food I ate, what I drank, how much I drank, and my sleep routine. It was an all-inclusive plan. God was teaching me how to take care of my body, His holy temple (1 Corinthians 6:19). The running was bringing me to a place where my mind was settled, and He could influence my thoughts.

Before moving to the property, I had always lived in the suburbs. I was immersed in people's ideas about how I should and should not live my life. Some of these influences were of God, and some were of the spirit of the world. As a young Christian, I had little discernment to know which voices were from God. Suddenly, all the influences stopped, and I was left alone in the woods with nothing but my thoughts and God. He began to train my brain.

At the time, I was reading "The Message" version of the Bible. I found I could identify with the language used. It flowed more like a story, and I began to recognize my own story through the words written on the page. God taught me that if I could worry, I could meditate on His Word. He replaced my fleshly thoughts with things from above (Colossians 3:12). He taught me to recognize when my thoughts were becoming toxic, when they were a burden to my soul, and when to change my mind to what was right (Philippians 4:8). Through the Bible, He taught me what His thoughts are, and I began to see through a new lens. I would struggle through my own thoughts until I found the truth. In this way, I could throw out the lies polluting my mind. I learned the world's knowledge carried fear and condemnation, but God's knowledge was a relief because it opened a way to peace and joy. I was new to spiritual discernment, and it took considerable quiet time with the Lord. The deliverance from oppressive lies brought incredible freedom so I was drawn to God's presence.

As a result of accepting God's thoughts and believing Him, thanksgiving rose from my inner parts. This type of response to God's personal Word is seen throughout the Bible. David would express deep worship and praise through the Psalms, writing clear expressions of thanksgiving during some of the most difficult trials of his life. Mary exploded in a magnificent song of worship in Luke 1:46–55. The Lord puts His joy in His servants, puts a new song in their mouth, and His praise comes forth. I began to *feel* how good God is. I began to thank Him verbally for any good thing in my day whether I thought God had anything to do with it or not. Some days, it was more of a discipline, using thanksgiving to replace my dismal thoughts. Through the discipline of giving thanks, I began to believe all good things came from Him. Joy bubbled up like a fountain within.

Perhaps the most profound way God used the wilderness to train me was to teach me about His will. John 4:34 (ESV) says, "Jesus said to them, 'My food is to do the will of him who sent me and to accomplish his work.'" Jesus is speaking on a spiritual level, and the food He speaks of nourishes abundant life. Jesus came to live in physical form to show us how to live life completely in sync with God through the Holy Spirit. We cannot experience His presence, His pleasure, and His supernatural power without obedience to the Holy Spirit. Throughout the Old Testament, the prophets wrote that God would put His law within our heart, and the Holy Spirit would reveal His law to each of us in a very personal way. God desires to have an intimate relationship in which He can speak to us about the details of our life.

Often, we see God's will as a destination, something to be found and hit like a target. However, I was beginning to see His will as a way, or a flow. He is a living and breathing God, constantly moving in our midst. I began to think about His Spirit as a steady moving train. I had the opportunity, even obligation, to move and flow with Him. I found that I could hop on and enjoy the ride or hop off and act independently. It was when I tried to do it on my own that I experienced loneliness, guilt, fear, and other feelings of separation. When I was doing life with Him, according to the prompting and empowerment of the Holy Spirit, I experienced peace, joy, and satisfaction in life. We are spiritual beings, and all of us have the capacity to sense His presence and to be led by Him. I was becoming more and more sensitive to the Holy Spirit.

God used my anxiety and sensitive nature to train me to move with the Holy Spirit in obedience as a lifestyle. He was teaching me to worship Him in every moment of my life. Learning to follow His promptings was a bit mechanical at first. I would get going in my day, doing my thing; and when anxiety swelled, I would stop and submit to God. I would ask Him what He would have me do in that moment and listen for His answer. During these early stages, it would simply be an inclination, or leaning, on my heart. Like most people, I didn't know for sure if this was God or my own desires; but with a teachable heart and willing spirit, I remained open to whichever direction He was leading. I trusted He would redirect me if I erred.

Once I began to recognize His promptings, He would give me small tasks. He'd prompt me to drop someone a note or invite a stranger to join us on a ride at Kings Island. It's these little things the Lord uses to teach us to recognize His prompting and to live according to His will. One day, I even followed His leading on country roads and was delighted when I arrived at my destination without getting lost! As we mature, we simply flow in Him naturally, and the relationship becomes less mechanical.

One thing I had to let go of was the need to understand. I had to be willing to make a mistake, and I had to put down my natural tendency to argue. With a logical mind, I had developed a habit of reasoning away His promptings when it didn't make sense. I had to resist the fear that caused me to tell God, "I can't, and here's why." Fear and pride had become stumbling blocks that caused me to disobey. I was fearful of what people would think and fearful of looking dumb. I needed to get over myself in order to do God's will. With great joy, I found understanding often came after obedience. Once I understood God's perspective, the thoughts of other people began to lose their grip on me. God is more interested in trust. Wisdom and insight into His ways flow in abundance as a result of obedience to the Holy Spirit.

The anxiety was an indication that I wasn't walking with God in my new nature. Not only does He tell us what to do, but also, He shows us how to do it. In this way, it is His strength that fuels our action. Depending on our personality and individual tendencies, we may be inclined to run ahead of God. Often, we receive direction only to hurry and make it happen by our own effort. We exhaust ourselves trying to do God's will and experience burnout as a result. In this way, we work for God and not with God. I was learning to lean my entire being into Him, allowing Him to empower me to live my life. My own nature was broken by sin; I only wanted to do life in Him. I learned to walk at His pace, not the frantic pace of the world. I found I had plenty of energy to do what I needed to do, simply by humbly submitting to His way continually.

As I enjoyed His presence, His comfort, and His peace, I craved to do His will more and more. The temptation to do my own thing melted away as I experienced a whole new way of living, a way filled with the things my soul truly longed for. I could taste and see for myself that the Lord was good, and my fleshly desires were increasingly less appealing. I was becoming more focused and attached to the Spirit of God.

Since I am prone to anxiety by nature, the only way to experience freedom in everyday life is to live out of my new nature. While our sin nature has been crucified with Christ on the cross, the residual effects of sin still reside in our flesh. The way to abundant life is to live out of our renewed spirit. God replaces our DNA with Christ's, and we walk into our new nature by being led and empowered by the Holy Spirit. God's Spirit trains us into realizing our unbroken fellowship with God, and we experience the abundance of new life in Christ.

This does not mean I live a life completely void of all anxiety. There are times when the Lord is dealing with me or preparing me for something, and I feel a similar heaviness. But this leaning is from God and produces righteousness. I still feel anxiety as the stress of this world presses into my soul, but I don't stay there. We remain sensitive to our old nature and the way of the world, but in Christ, we now have a different option. We are no longer bound to our natural way but can choose to walk in a new way.

Lord, in so many ways, I find myself in the space between Your promise and fulfillment. Take my circumstances and use them for your purpose. Help me see and understand what you are doing in and around me during this period. Encourage me in my faith, allowing me to see Your promises as reality, fostering patience within. Reveal to me when I have been disobedient, acting according to my own will. I submit to Your way. Use my internal and external struggles to purify me and teach me to walk in the Spirit.

Chapter 5

True Identity

Loved. Forgiven. Accepted. Precious. Special. Enough. Chosen. Victorious. This is who we are as a son or daughter of God, yet often our feelings and behavior reveal a different story. When we walk around discouraged, believing we are anything other than a child of God, we aren't enjoying the benefits of our identity Christ died to give us.

Once faith enters a heart, God begins to reveal our true identity and His purpose for us in His kingdom. Only God knows who He made us to be and reveals it to us personally through an intimate relationship with Himself. This revelation comes through time and experience with God. Let's take a look at Simon Peter's story in Matthew 16:15–18 (NLT):

> Then he asked them, "But who do you say I am?"
>
> Simon Peter answered, "You are the Messiah, the Son of the living God."
>
> Jesus replied, "You are blessed, Simon son of John, because my Father in heaven has revealed this to you. You

> did not learn this from any human being. Now I say to you that you are Peter (which means 'rock'), and upon this rock I will build my church, and all the powers of hell will not conquer it."

What may not be apparent is that no earthly authority was proclaiming Jesus as Messiah at the time of Simon Peter's admission. The church didn't recognize Jesus, but a strange man named John (Matthew 3) who lived in the wilderness did. The leaders weren't confirming Jesus. Simon knew this information only because his faith in God revealed it. When Jesus saw his genuine faith, He was able to reveal Simon's true name and God's intended purpose for his life. He called him by his name and that name indicated purpose. Peter would be a stone in the foundation of the church or, in other words, a founding father. On the surface, Peter didn't look anything like a rock. We read he was impetuous, outspoken, and even denied knowing Jesus. But in time, through God's influence, Peter was able to walk in his true identity and have God's desired effect in the church, on the world, and in His kingdom.

As we spend intimate time in God's presence, connecting with His Spirit in our spirit, God begins to reveal our calling. We are all called a son or daughter of the King, and each has a unique place in His kingdom. A calling is God's invitation to participate in Christ's redemptive work. There are many parts in the body of Christ, and we must all do our part or the whole body suffers. Each of us is special and critical to God's plan for the earth and His kingdom. This world misses out on God's glory in us when we don't know who we are or for what purpose we were created. Only God can reveal this calling.

Notice Jesus didn't give any specific details about circumstances when He revealed Peter's true identity. Who we are in Christ, who we were made to be, is independent of circumstances. Our identity may lead us into a specific vocation, but a vocation doesn't define who we are. We are who we are in Christ no matter where we are or what we are doing. God reveals Himself in everything we do. When we know who we are from God's perspective, the doing comes naturally. Our true identity indicates our calling, which indicates what we are to do for all eternity in His kingdom on earth and in heaven.

As we walk in the nature Christ put in us the moment we received the faith to believe, we experience abundant life. When we accept God's calling on our life, it is then we experience the richness and fulfillment for which our heart longs. We understand our purpose and are compelled by the Spirit to do what we do. Our satisfaction comes from within and is not dependent on what we do or what happens in this world.

First Samuel 16:7 says, "For the Lord sees not as man sees; for man looks at the outward appearance, but the Lord looks at the heart." Personality tests and spiritual inventories may be able to assess what is visible on the outside, but God is revealing what is deeper within the heart. These tests can show what is on the exterior of a person's nature or what the Spirit has already manifested, but the results are a glimmer of the reality of our true nature.

As a young married person, I struggled to see Casey for who he really was. Like many newlyweds, we fought to figure out how to do life together. God made us one, but we weren't sure what that looked like in everyday life, and we were both hurt in the struggle. I realized my pain was tainting the way I was seeing my husband; my perspective of him was distorted. I began to pray that God would open my eyes to see Casey the way He sees him. What I saw was surprising and hard for us both to believe.

God was showing me that Casey was a leader. He has been given a quiet strength and leads from an inner fortitude. Because Casey is an introvert with a gentle personality, he had not been recognized as a leader by this world. He himself was convinced he was a helper by nature. I began to treat Casey as the leader God was revealing, and I began to trust his leadership. The respect God was calling me to give my husband came naturally as I believed His perspective. We began to understand how we fit together as man and wife by understanding our own identities in Christ.

Once God reveals our true identity, He uses our circumstances to confirm His word through our obedience. In the years after we received revelation about who Casey was from God's perspective, He used a very unique work situation to establish this truth in the reality of his life. In an incredible act of faith, Casey felt prompted by the Holy Spirit to quit his job. We had no plan, three children, and a house; but we knew it was the right thing to do. What happened after was nothing short of extraordinary. Coworkers and superiors poured out kind words and affirmation. Because of such strong reactions among managers, human resources met with Casey and gave him an opportunity to speak about the work environment in his department. The company responded, and God used Casey's leadership to change the atmosphere in his workplace. Casey was asked to stay, and God brought His good purpose and blessing to the company through Casey's obedience.

By spending intimate time in the wilderness with God, I began to see myself differently. God was revealing my true nature and for what purpose He created me. He began to whisper things that were challenging my way of thinking. I had been taught certain principles in the church about how God works. These quiet whispers were blowing up my religious box. I searched the Scripture for validity of what God was placing on my heart. I couldn't find any passages that said God no longer works in that way or that particular gifts were no longer dispensed or that women could not possess certain callings.

"My child," God spoke to my heart, "fear has caused man to attempt to control Me and My Spirit. But I cannot be controlled by man." He was encouraging me to believe Him.

"You are My prophetess."

I found this alarming since I came from a doctrinal background which taught cessationism, a belief that the revelatory and miraculous gifts have ceased. I recalled as a child I would have knowledge of things I shouldn't have known and how that knowledge caused me to speak, minister, serve, or pray. When I was young, I didn't question these things; but as an adult, I had begun to suppress the Spirit's work in my life.

When our parents or spiritual leaders fail to recognize our true identity early in our lives, we can be encouraged in a way that is contrary to God's will. When this happens, it is difficult to believe God when He begins to reveal Himself in an intimate and personal way. We must allow the Father to reveal Himself as He truly is. I became acquainted with His true character through reading the Bible in its entirety. Once we begin to see God more clearly, we can understand ourselves more clearly. Often, His perspective of who we are is contrary to the information and confirmation we have received by this world. Many have worked to please man rather than our Heavenly Father (Galatians 1:10). Our disobedience creates a wound in our heart or hardness toward the Father and His purpose for our lives.

The spiritual gift of discernment was becoming so acute in my life that I could be listening to a person speak yet hear something completely different in my spirit. I wasn't sure what was happening or why I was hearing things that not even the person speaking had yet realized. Confusion would turn to doubt as the person would deny the truth God was speaking to my heart.

I walked the paths of our property, wrestling God as Jacob wrestled (Genesis 32:22–32). I have always had a tenacity about my relationship with God, causing me to dig and dig until finding peace. This was one such time. God was revealing Himself in a way I had not yet seen or experienced, and it was hard to believe.

Toward the middle of our ten years on the property, there began rumblings in the neighborhood. Tensions were rising, and there was talk of a civil lawsuit among neighbors. I had nothing but love in my heart for the two families involved and sought the Lord about my response to this situation. I believed that He wanted me to continue loving and serving both, but I had the impression that one of the women would put a restraining order on me. Oh! How I was filled with fear. I had not yet accepted or surrendered to God's calling on my life. I felt so strongly she would put a restraining order on me that I shared my fears with two different small groups. Everything in my flesh was telling me to run from the situation! Earthly reason told me to run from this woman! God was telling me to love her and continue ministering to her.

The day came when restraining orders were tossed casually against neighbors, and indeed, this woman obtained a temporary restraining order against me. It was as though I could visually see a demonic spirit on her shoulder, whispering delusions that she repeated to the judge. I was God's voice of truth in this woman's life, and Satan needed to shut me up! I knew in my heart that this was a test. In fact, looking back, I can see it was my calling being tested. There was absolutely nothing on earth I could do to save or wiggle my way out of this situation, so I bowed in submission and said, "Have Your way, Lord. I will do it Your way."

His Spirit poured into and out of me during those tumultuous months. I could feel His Presence resting on my shoulders in a tangible way. When I read the Bible, it was as though I was seeing right through the Word to see His reality here on earth and in my life. I was amazed at the closeness I felt to David in the Psalms as he expressed the exact feelings I was experiencing. The encouragement I received from the Lord flowed effortlessly into those around me. I was a free-flowing conduit for God's Word. I ministered to the other woman involved in the lawsuit, held powerful prayer meetings in our home, and baptized my son during this period. It was as though I could actually see what the Spirit was doing, that my sight was somehow sharpened to see His work here on earth. It was awe-inspiring. I was operating in my calling simply by clinging to Jesus. When under pressure, we see what we are made of, the good and the bad. God was proving my true identity by my circumstances. I began returning to the innocent faith of my childhood.

This renewed faith altered the spirit of our home and seeped into my family members. God's power was changing Casey and softening his heart to my calling. I believed DJ's baptism was a natural result of the Spirit's supernatural work in our home. It is a moment he and I will never forget when he put his faith together and said, "Well, why shouldn't I be baptized?"

"Great! I'll talk to the church right away," I said.

However, like the Ethiopian eunuch (Acts 8:36–38), DJ was thinking right away, in our creek! I performed the baptism with his little sister and brother as witnesses. I saw the Holy Spirit come over my son, and he ran to share what had just happened to our not-yet-believing neighbor. DJ described the experience as a miracle. He wrote in his journal, "I finilly had a maricl in my life. I was happy to be a Chisin. When I was baptizd, I felt my gifts." He also wrote,

"The best part was that I felt thankful for evrything." When he came out of the water, he described that the world seemed brighter and more vibrant. He was experiencing true spiritual awakening.

The test of the restraining order was not easy. I wasn't perfect and didn't walk through the trial confident in my faith. I was scared. It was my word against hers, and my fate would be determined by the opinion of a judge. In addition to the temporary restraining order, she had also filed a violation, which is a federal offense. If charged, it would alter the way I would live the rest of my life. I was unsure of the outcome, but I submitted to the Lord's plan.

Just as Joseph was put in jail for something he didn't do in Genesis 39, my circumstance didn't make sense, and it certainly wasn't fair. If you don't know Joseph's full story, please pause and read it in Genesis 37, 39–45. As a child, God gave Joseph dreams that revealed he was destined for great leadership. Even though Joseph was sold into slavery and later put in jail, God caused him success in all that he did and gave him more and more leadership responsibilities. Joseph knew God was with him, not only giving him the ability to do well in his everyday life but also giving him supernatural ability. God had given him the interpretation of dreams that eventually led to the manifestation of His will for Joseph.

God desires to express His supernatural gifts in all His children. As Christians, we have the Holy Spirit in us and therefore have access to His divine nature (2 Peter 1:4). In Him, we possess the gifts of the Spirit, including the prophetic and revelatory gifts of God. It is when we allow these gifts to arise and flow into our circumstances that we realize He is the one empowering us to live in extraordinary ways. We all have access to heavenly knowledge and wisdom, and He speaks to us about the future as though it has already occurred. Through believing His word, we draw His truth into our life here and now.

During the time of the restraining order, God began to speak to my heart that the case would be dropped. I didn't know how the details would unfold, but I believed Him. Like Joseph, I could sense He was with me and it gave me confidence to trust His plan. I began to push worry aside and live my life in peace. I began to look beyond the fear and pressure of the accusations against me. By spending time with my childhood best friend, God reminded me I was not the person they were accusing me of being. We have an opportunity in Christ to walk in peace even while experiencing incomprehensible trials. I rested in His presence and trusted His hand. The Amplified version of Hebrews 10:23 says, "So let us seize and hold fast and retain without wavering the hope we cherish and confess and our acknowledgment of it, for He Who promised is reliable (sure) and faithful to His word." We have an opportunity to actually seize hope, a heavenly reality, and hold it as true (a fact) in our earthly reality. Our hope becomes tangible as we grasp God's promises and live them out in our lives. God is faithful and always true to His word, whether written in the Bible or spoken to us personally by the Holy Spirit. Believing His Word settled the issue in my heart.

I knew God was with me in a real way by the comfort He provided through the people around me. Neighbors enveloped me in love, expressing concern and helping in any way they could. I felt supported in their acts of kindness, whether it be through mowing the sides of our driveway, watching the children while I met with the lawyer, or just simply being present in my home when the police came to report the accusations against me. My parents, desiring to rescue me from afar, paid my legal fees.

If we understand our life now to be a training ground for eternity, we can see why God allows difficult circumstances to test us. In the Bible, God went great lengths to catch the attention of His servants. He does what it takes to bring us into His will and purpose for our lives. God allows us to go through various trials, not to prove ourselves to Him, but to prove our true identity to ourselves. He gives us opportunities to let our faith spring forth into action, causing us to believe, walk in His way, and see who we really are. Much growth occurred in Joseph through his years as a slave and inmate. God used his leadership in slavery and prison long before elevating him to second in command of Egypt. Joseph himself recognized the importance of testing and put his brothers through a series of tests in Genesis 42–45 in order to produce the fruit of righteousness in their lives. Much growth occurred in me through the restraining order as God revealed Himself in a powerful way. When we have these types of experiences with His Spirit, it causes a greater level of trust, and we are able to walk more freely in our true identity. I am a child of God whose purpose is to teach and equip the body of Christ with the prophetic gifts. What Satan intended to use to destroy me was actually making me stronger in Christ.

The case dragged on for months. My lawyer scheduled a deposition, but my accuser did not respond. The deposition was rescheduled for the first day of school, the day I had hoped and believed the case would be resolved. Early in the morning, minutes before school started, I received word the restraining order was dropped.

Using very unique and personal circumstances, God confirmed His calling on my life. He does the same with each of us. I'm fairly certain not many of you have found yourselves under a restraining order, but God meets us where we are in extraordinary ways. He will custom-tailor your life to reach and affirm you according to His will. When we look for God and are sensitive to His Spirit, He speaks our true identity and communicates His purpose for creating us. Through obedience, He confirms His word in our life and circumstances.

Father, I release who the world says I am. I surrender who I think I am or who my parents say I should be. Allow me to see myself from Your perspective and help me to believe You. Please confirm me in my identity in my life and circumstances.

Chapter 6

Inside Out, Upside Down

Transformed life in Christ, as defined by the Bible (Romans 12:2), is a changed life from the ways of the world to a life that pleases God. When we receive Christ's life, we are declared righteous and holy in Him. Transformation is the process by which the truth about us in our inward spirit becomes apparent in our outward appearance and actions. This is not a superficial change by conforming to a set of external standards of behavior, but a spiritual renewal that manifests itself in outward actions. Transformation results in holiness as demonstrated by being led and empowered by the Holy Spirit. Christian obedience is designed to reveal more of God's nature and character in us. We become increasingly aware of His presence and begin to co-labor (2 Corinthians 6:1) with Him. He prompts and empowers our actions, and our fears melt into His love for us. In this way, we increasingly reflect the glory of Christ and His righteousness.

To understand spiritual maturity, we can observe the growth of a child. When a child is young, he submits to the authority of his parents. He obeys the rules and is trained by them. These rules are intended to keep the child safe until he gains wisdom and understanding and is able to conduct himself rightly when the boundaries have been removed. Paul describes the law in Galatians 3:24-26 (NASB) as our trainer. He writes, "Therefore the Law has become our tutor to lead us to Christ, so that we may be justified by faith. But now that faith has come, we are no longer under a tutor. For you are all sons of God through faith in Christ Jesus."

When we are young in our faith, we innocently follow what we see written in the Bible or what we hear from our spiritual leaders. These boundaries keep us safe within the way of righteousness. As we submit to these external instructions, the Holy Spirit is able to reveal more of God's heart. This causes a transformation from our old, hardened heart into a tender one that is sensitive and responsive to the Holy Spirit (Ezekiel 11:19). Our heart becomes more like God's heart and our new heart is able to sense and see God in this world. Following Him becomes as natural as it once was to follow the way of the world.

Man in his natural way does the right thing and hopes it means he is right with God. The flesh works from the outside, but God's way is opposite. God is the one who puts truth in our inner being, and He is the one who changes us from the inside. Psalm 51:10 (ESV) says, "Create in me a clean heart, O God, and renew a right spirit within me." Transformation occurs when this right spirit is allowed to work outward. God is working to restore our soul and body back into harmony, enabling us to worship Him "in spirit and in truth (reality)" (John 4:24 AMP). That which is true of us in our spirit becomes the reality of what is seen on the outside. More often than not, Christians have a hard time believing what God says about them because it doesn't seem to match reality. What they see on the outside isn't what God sees on the inside. The Spirit desires to restore us, making us a whole and united person. Remember, our identity in Christ is righteous and holy; true hypocrisy occurs when we don't act like it.

Without spiritual transformation, we cannot please God even though we appear to be doing all the right things. It is common for those who are young in Christ to focus on what they see with their natural eyes. Before God reveals spiritual truth, human reality is what can be physically observed by the five senses. An ordinary conclusion is to measure transformation by what is seen on the outside and fall prey to the performance trap. We take what we read in the Bible on a surface level and receive (spiritual) encouragement according to the flesh, quickly deriving a list of external expectations. We use these expectations to measure ourselves and others. We believe the myth that we need to do certain things and avoid others in order to please God.

In Genesis 4, both Cain and Abel brought offerings to the Lord. Cain brought the fruit of his harvest because he was a farmer. Abel brought a sheep because he was a shepherd. Both desired to please God by bringing Him a gift. However, God respected Abel's offering but not Cain's. If we peel back the layers of theology, beyond the required sacrifice of shed blood, we see it was Cain's heart that God judged. In Hebrews 11:4, we learn it was Abel's faith that pleased God; but 1 John 3:12 tells us Cain was of the evil one, which is the spirit of this world and of the flesh. This evil was later revealed in the act of killing Able. Whether or not we do well, acting righteously, was and always is about the faith of the giver.

From the moment we first believe, Satan fights to keep us in darkness. If he can't withhold us from God's kingdom, he grapples to destroy our abundant life and diminish our effectiveness. He sends a religious spirit to distract us from realizing the relationship God desires. This is the thief in the sheepfold Jesus referred to in John 10:10. Religion and relationship were never intended to be separated. Sin in the flesh causes the divide, and man in his own effort performs religious duty independent of God's will. The religious spirit is characterized by fear and can look like obedience to Christ, but is performed in the power of the person's flesh.

The religious spirit is what Jesus publicly revealed in the Pharisees. Church leaders had put a heavy yoke of rules and regulations on the Jews. Judaism had morphed from true religion into a set of man-made, culture-oriented dictates of the flesh. This false religion sucked the very life out of God's people. The religious spirit is venomous, spitting hate and spewing judgment. It is of Satan and comes straight from hell. It hates abundant life and weighs God's people down with guilt, condemnation, and crippling fear. This spirit is a master of disguise and hides behind pride. Most don't realize they are being influenced and controlled by this life-stealing spirit.

Saul was oppressed by the religious spirit in Acts. Chapter eight states Saul not only consented to Stephen's brutal murder by the Jews because of his faith in Jesus but also was pleased and fully approving. *Pleased.* An innocent man had been stoned in a dramatic, bloody display, and Saul was pleased. He continued in this shameful way until God got hold of his heart and transformed him into Paul, an incredible ambassador for Christ and author of much of the New Testament.

People who are weighed down by the religious spirit do all the right things but are not experiencing love and acceptance in Christ. They "have to" get up early to read their Bible and pray, they "have to" serve in the church, and they "have to" tithe. Their good works are accomplished out of duty, obligation, and fear of judgment. Worried about religious disapproval, they avoid engaging in culture and avoid participating in worldly things. Because they carry a sense of judgment, they breathe judgment on those who do not live up to their religious standards. Pride in their ability to do right and avoid wrong causes them to carry an air of superiority while constantly fearing judgment and condemnation for what they do or don't do.

True transformation occurs when God is allowed to guide our mind and emotions that inform our will and cause us to act righteously. In this way, not only do we find God's will, but also our will becomes God's will! This type of transformation requires spiritual training. The Spirit trains our thoughts, our emotions, and our will to be like Christ. Through an intimate relationship with Him, God's thoughts become our thoughts, His emotions become our emotions, and His will becomes our will. What begins in our spirit, permeates our soul, until finally expressing itself in our life and world. This is a holy makeover as we allow God to influence our entire being.

First Corinthians 2:16 (NIV) explains, "we have the mind of Christ," and it is the role of the Holy Spirit to reveal Christ's thoughts to us in a personal way. The Spirit intercedes to teach us what God thinks about our everyday life. God continually uses the Bible to teach me the mind of Christ. Early in my spiritual training, I would "see" God's thoughts written in the Bible. As I read, the Word opened like a flower, and I could "hear" God speaking into my personal situation through the words on the page. I journaled these Bible-inspired thoughts and found myself praying through scripture and rewriting passages in the first person. The written Word was becoming personal through these exercises as I was growing in my relationship with Christ.

After years of praying through scripture in an intimate way and changing my thoughts to match God's thoughts, I began to hear His voice within my spirit. Just as we recognize the voice of our earthly dad and can "hear" his voice long after we have left home, I began to hear the voice of my Heavenly Father. Having lived with my dad for eighteen years, I learned his thoughts. I had taken many of his thoughts as my own. I knew how he would feel about certain situations and knew how he would react because of years of experience with him. The same is true with our Heavenly Father. As we spend intimate time with Him, allowing Him to speak personal words into our life and our situation, we begin to take on His thoughts. This causes a complete change in perspective. We begin to see this world through a faithful perspective, the same perspective that inspired the writers of the Bible. He causes us to come out of our small mind to see things from a higher view.

Without the guidance of the Holy Spirit, our fleshly thoughts get in the way of obedience to God. So many of us have a wealth of information about God, but we don't know Him intimately. We study Him like a subject but never get to know Him as a friend. There is a temptation to take pride in what we know about God and act in our own knowledge. This is in essence the fall of man. Adam and Eve took the fruit of knowledge and acted in their own will. Their eyes were opened to good and evil; and they became their own god, their own lord, and made decisions accordingly. The Israelites made the same mistake when they demanded a king to rule over the nation (1 Samuel 8). They took their eyes off God who was their King and Lord and desired a man to rule them like other nations.

Knowledge of good and evil ultimately cost Saul, the man anointed to become Israel's first king, the kingdom. In First Samuel 10, the prophet Samuel anointed Saul and gave him specific instructions from the Lord. When Samuel didn't come when expected, Saul knew what needed to be done and did it himself. Saul offered the burned offering without

Samuel, an act that was forbidden (1 Samuel 13:12). Saul's disobedience evolved into deception and rebellion. Samuel rebuked Saul and said, "Has the LORD as great delight in burnt offerings and sacrifices, as in obeying the voice of the LORD? Behold, to obey is better than sacrifice, and to listen than the fat of rams" (1 Samuel 15:22 ESV). In other words, God was saying, "You do what you think is right based on your own knowledge and will. I'm more concerned about you obeying my voice. I am God, not you." This is how knowledge causes us to stumble—when knowledge leads us to judge and act for ourselves.

When I made the choice to go into engineering, I trusted my own reason and logic for guidance. Ultimately, I based my decision on intellectual facts rather than God's impression on my heart. Looking back, I can see in my spirit I was saying to God, "I will do what You want, but first I'm going to do what I want." I did what I thought was right based on my own knowledge and will, but my feelings were telling another story. Our feelings can be a check and balance and can indicate when our unrenewed mind leads us astray.

We are created in the image of God (Genesis 1:27), and like God, we have feelings. He created us to be sensitive beings, and this is good. Emotions are an important part of the soul that Christ came to save and is resurrecting for the kingdom of God. The Amplified version of 1 Corinthians 2:16 explains that not only do we have the mind of Christ, but also, we hold the thoughts of His heart, which includes feelings and purposes. Just as we take hold of the thoughts of God, we also take on the feelings and desires of God. God is renewing our mind and thereby renewing our emotions. The good news is the gospel works with our emotions, and the harvest of our soul includes our feelings.

Growing up, I was taught you can't trust feelings and shouldn't make decisions based on emotion. I learned that I shouldn't let my emotions control my actions and that I had to do certain things even if I didn't feel like it. I learned certain emotions were bad, and I shouldn't feel that way. While all of this was partially true, in my childhood perception, I mistakenly believed my emotions were wrong. Therefore, I thought, the whole point was to avoid the wrong emotions! While I couldn't always control my circumstances, I thought I could control the way I felt. The dilemma was that I did feel those "wrong" emotions. My flesh did what it does, it fought for preservation. In order to survive, I simply ignored the bad feelings. I became proficient at not allowing myself to feel pain and declaring happiness instead. I thought that was joy! Unfortunately, when we start denying our emotions, we also deny the Holy Spirit access into our emotional life. I had no chance of experiencing transformation in the realm of emotions as long as I refused to acknowledge my feelings.

We cannot divide the mind, will, and emotions. We cannot feed and take care of one, ignore the other, and expect to have a healthy soul. God intended us to be a whole being, and we are designed to function with continual interaction between each part. The practice of denying emotions proved to be incredibly unhealthy. I'm a very sensitive person, and my heart was growing harder and harder as I stored hidden pain away from the influence of the Holy Spirit. Soon my life became about managing stress. Although I once was a care-free child, the burdens of adult life were crushing me. I consumed self-help books and learned what the experts said I needed to do to take care of my body and soul. One particular afternoon, I was terribly upset about a situation with a woman at church. I called a friend to vent, but the battery on my phone died. I went for a vigorous run to work out my emotion, but I twisted my ankle. I ended up flat on the bed, with an ankle throbbing, and crying out to God. "What do You want from me?"

He quietly whispered in my spirit, "I want you."

From that day forward, God trained me to go to Him with my emotions. Instead of venting to my husband, complaining to a friend, or calling my mom, He trained me to tell Him how I was feeling. I did this through journaling. At first, I would write furiously, my words seeping with judgment. But the more time I spent in His presence, the less my nasty attitude remained. He gently turned my eyes from myself to Him. I learned to receive His thoughts about my situation, and my emotions would turn to match His. When we begin to see our life and world from God's perspective, His feelings flood our soul. I learned God works with my thoughts, stirring emotions based on truth, which propel me into obedience. This can be described as intuition or "gut feeling," and these feelings help us obey God even before we are able to recognize His voice in our spirit.

We all have a conscience that leads and guides us in this world even before we trust God to be Lord of our life. The Spirit often leans on our conscience in order to guide us into repentance and obedience. It is common for Christians to express uncertainty and confusion when trying to discern God's will. It is natural for us to question, is this me or Him? Is this my will or His? I have even heard well-meaning Christians express, "I just wish I could see the writing on the wall." In essence, this is our flesh desiring to remain under the Old Testament Law when God's expectations were written and followed externally through Moses' connection to God. We all have this special connection and access to God through the blood of Christ. It is Satan who says, "That wasn't God," and causes us to dismiss His voice. When we explain away God's voice and promptings for fear and doubt, our heart becomes calloused. Our disobedience causes us to become dull to His Spirit. Confusion increases and clarity decreases.

God is interested in trust. He desires us to believe Him at His Word. The Bible says that we have been made new, and we have the opportunity to believe it. Part of maturing is being willing to trust our conscience, not because we believe in ourselves, but because we believe in Christ. We step out in our uncertainty, trusting God's Spirit to corral us, without condemnation, if we have made a mistake. Sometimes, it takes a conscious effort to release guilt, not allowing it to control us because we know it is not from God. Perhaps it means taking a risk, causing us to feel out of control. At times, it may appear as though God's way is upside down, contrary to what we think or feel is the right way. He is training us to go with the flow of His Spirit, ever increasing our sensitivity as we obey His prompting. It is through obedience that we personally taste and see that the Lord is good, realizing we don't want to live without Him!

With an open and teachable spirit, we step out, willing to be redirected if necessary. We trust our thoughts and feelings because we trust God is influencing and transforming them. We learn to recognize Him and feel His presence. We can sense when we are acting independently in the flesh and crave to step back into His will. It is in this type of relationship we realize our true depravity and inability to live without Him. His presence brings us so much joy and fulfillment that we desire to go where God goes, moving only when He moves.

If obedience comes from an internal transformation by the Holy Spirit, you may be wondering what our connection is to what the Bible describes as the law or external standards and expectations of behavior that remind us of Old Testament Law. This world operates based on standards of performance. When we are young, we are required to meet our parents' standard of behavior or we get in trouble. In school, it is necessary to make the grade or we fail. In sports, we win or we lose. In our job, we meet performance expectations or are fired. Even in church, we are told what we should and should not do as a Christian. We are constantly measured by our performance. It may be difficult to grasp that God's way is inside out and upside down from the way of the world.

Jesus said in Matthew 5:17 (NLT), "I did not come to abolish the Law of Moses or the writings of the prophets." Yet Paul writes in Romans 7:6 (NLT), "But now we have been released from the law, for we died to it and are no longer captive to its power." The law remains, yet we are no longer bound by it. To be bound by something means to be under its influence or control. The law carries with it an unspoken judgment. If someone hears, "You should not chew gum," the person chewing gum automatically feels judged. It's not the person giving the law who makes the judgment, but the law itself. When we hear, "You should not chew gum," we may feel morally obligated to follow or we may feel angry over the injustice of the rule. We may feel guilty or unworthy if we are unable to meet the expectation. Or we may feel compelled to obey for fear of being judged. If the law, through standards and expectations, causes us to feel unworthy, I say, "Praise the Lord!" The law kills the spirit behind self-righteousness because it shows us we are not enough. It is for all of this that Christ came to die!

What Jesus and Paul are communicating is that, yes, in this world, there are laws and standards of behavior. However, in Christ, we are no longer under legal obligation to meet these external moral standards to gain approval. According to Him, we are already forgiven and find favor with God. We are freed from the self-righteousness of meeting these expectations and freed from the condemnation of missing the mark. We are no longer devoted or attached to external rules; the rules don't rule us. Does this make us lawless citizens? No, not in God's kingdom nor on earth. But rather, we serve a higher purpose. Paul continues in verse 6 (NLT), "Now we can serve God, not in the old way of obeying the letter of the law, but in the new way of living in the Spirit." We are ruled by the Holy Spirit. When we live by the Spirit, we are living out the intent of the Old Testament Law. This is the same purpose Jesus communicated when He was on earth. We are compelled and obligated to the Spirit who is revealing God's law written on our heart.

We can consider the old and new covenants a way or manner of relating to God. Under the old covenant, the Jews followed God's commands given by the High Priest. These commands formed the Law. Since Christ came and died, He established a new covenant in which we each become priests and receive God's instruction directly through the Holy Spirit. Paul describes the new covenant in 2 Corinthians 3 as a dispensation of the Spirit that causes us to obtain and be governed by the Holy Spirit instead of an external written code. Paul writes in 2 Corinthians 3:17 (NLT), "For the Lord is the Spirit, and wherever the Spirit of the Lord is, there is freedom." What is absolutely phenomenal about this freedom is that we are now free to obey the law.

Peter describes a godly attitude toward the law of the land in his letter to the churches in the northern part of Asia Minor. First Peter 2:13 (NIV) says, "Submit yourselves for the Lord's sake to every human authority." He continues in verse 16, "Live as free people, but do not use your freedom as a cover-up for evil; live as God's slaves." We are free, but in Christ, it is impossible to use our freedom to sin. It can be most difficult to submit to authority we have judged unjust or even crooked. Our patient endurance glorifies God in the way Christ's undeserved sufferings glorified God. While he was abused and insulted, Jesus made no threats or retaliation, but trusted God who judges fairly.

In Galatians, Paul reproves believers for feeling obligated to meet certain standard as preached by Judaizers, who insisted Gentile converts abide by Jewish rites like circumcision. Yet he also had Timothy circumcised in Acts 16:3 in order to minister to people in lands where Jews were present. The key lies in Jesus's statement that He had not come to abolish the law. Jesus grew up abiding by the law of Judaism. It is in freedom that Jesus submitted to the religious system of the Jews. Similarly, Jesus freely submitted to the law of the land as indicated by His discussion about taxes in Matthew 22:17–21. When we are freed by the blood of Christ, He destroys the enmity (friction) between us and the law (Ephesians 3:15). Nobody likes to be told what to do and especially to be told what not to do. Human nature hates the law. In Christ, this hatred is removed, and we are no longer bothered or offended by the rules. We no longer feel obligated or manipulated by fear to obey. We freely put ourselves under the law of the land and the instructions of our spiritual leaders. We can do this because we know our worth is not tied to our ability to reach man's standards. It is for joy we submit to our leaders since there is no longer the burden of self-righteousness or condemnation.

The reality of God's presence is realized in obedience. God is present and so very close to each one of us. Christian obedience is when we submit to God's law written on our heart as revealed by the Holy Spirit. We obey by living a life according to the prompting and empowering of the Holy Spirit. As in the Old Testament, the law exists within God's presence. Exodus 25:10–22 gives us a beautiful description of the Ark of the Covenant. God commanded Moses to build a fantastic box made of acacia wood overlaid by pure gold. God told Moses to put the testimony, which was the ten commandments, in the box. Resting on top of the box was the mercy seat where the high priest would sprinkle the blood of sacrifice once a year. Above the mercy seat were two gold cherubim, creating the framework for God's visible presence to rest. It was here that God said to Moses in Exodus 25:22 (NASB), "There I will meet with you; and from above the mercy seat, from between the two cherubim which are upon the ark of the testimony, I will speak to you about all that I will give you in commandment for the sons of Israel." Today, when we obey, God's visible presence breaks through us into this world. We personally experience God through obedience, causing us to feel how very close He is.

The difference for those who follow Christ is that our gaze is not on the standard. Instead, we are focused on God's glory abiding in us. We are focused on obeying the Holy Spirit, and our minds are set on things above (Colossians 3:2). We are concentrated on learning from God how to do our work. Reaching the standard is simply a by-product of who we are rather than an end for our effort. In this way, a job well done is not measured by man's standard, but by our relationship to God. Obedience is a joyful adventure that allows us to feel God's favor and receive confirmation in this world. What is true in our spirit becomes true in the reality of our life.

The difference in perspective causes a change in motivation. When we are focused on earthly expectations, we can be self-motivated and rely on ourselves to reach the goal. This is why it can be so difficult to take when we miss the mark. Many have feelings of failure, shame, and embarrassment. These feelings are not coming from God, but rather are a result of our own pride and expectation.

In our imperfection, He perfects us by His love. I have learned that His way of perfection and the world's idea of perfection are two different things. The world's perfection is based on performance. God's manner of perfection is unbroken fellowship, which is already true in our spirit and has little to do with reaching outside standards. I learned I didn't need to worry about meeting people's expectations as long as I focused on living in Him. He was releasing me from the demands of culture and man's religion. Surprisingly, I discovered others were pleased when I kept my attention on God. When we move with the Spirit, obeying His promptings and doing life His way, perfection according to the world's standard may be the result but is not the objective. Perfection to God is when His servant does life with Him, bringing what is true in the spirit to the surface of everyday life.

Holiness, excellence, and perfection are just a natural result when our focus is on God in all that we do. Our expectation relies on God to be holy. Pursuing holiness is pursuing a relationship with God. The boundaries of the law keep us safe. The Holy Spirit would never guide us to do something explicitly defined as sin in the Bible. In fact, the human heart is prone to stray and the boundaries serve as a check. We cannot release the standards as Jesus indicated in Matthew 5:17, yet we are free to obey the will of the Father rather than adhere to a prescription of good behavior.

One year, I signed up for an intense Bible study. In my own mind, I thought this was a good and right thing to do. But there was a nagging sense I was going the wrong direction. I felt as though I was wandering through the study and the path was difficult. I struggled in my thoughts. Week nine of the study was about obedience, and I felt deeply convicted. I realized I was not obeying God but I didn't understand what He was asking me to do. It didn't make sense to me that He wouldn't want me to do the study. At the risk of my pride, I dropped out.

That night, I quieted myself in the Lord. I heard Him say, "I need your undivided attention right now. I am preparing you." God had previously prompted me to read a book called *Obedience Made Simple*, by Larry B. Reese, but I had put it off in order to do the Bible study. God was preparing me to enter Discipleship School, a ministry at our church in which Larry teaches and disciples students for one year. I affectionately dubbed it "Obedience School."

Father, please teach me what obedience means to You. Reveal to me how You are growing me from the inside to be more like You on the outside. Reveal how I have fallen into the performance trap and man's definition of perfection. Teach me to live upside down according to the world's standards, seeking instead to please You according to Your Spirit.

Chapter 7

Rooting Out the Enemy

One day, I took the children to a park to ride bikes and rollerblade. There weren't any sidewalks and the park was nearly empty, so we used the driveway for our activities. At times, the children would get ahead, and I would be unable to see them. *What if a car comes?* I feared. *What if someone abducts them?* And the mother of all fears, *What if someone rapes them?* I could feel Satan's terror. God was saying, "Trust me, Lisa," and I wanted to, but my feelings betrayed me.

The next weekend, I attended a women's conference for our church. One of the speakers was sharing the horrors she experienced as a child, including sexual abuse. My skin was crawling, and I had this terrible urge to run out of the room. I searched for an exit but found I was completely blocked in. I cried out to God, "I can't stand the evil!" It took great effort not to run. God answered, "You can't stand it because you are terrified."

The theme for the conference was Satan's strongholds. We were instructed to write our stumbling blocks on small stones. I wrote, "Fear," and quickly ran to the pastor's wife for prayer. She could see Satan's terror on me and boldly prayed against his spirit. God delivered me in those moments and I felt a huge relief; however, I instinctively knew I would need to walk in the newness of this freedom. I asked her to pray that I would never go back and drink from that lake of fear and death again.

We have spoken about the nature of the flesh and how God is working from the inside to influence our entire being so we can experience Christ's life and live abundantly in God's kingdom. We discussed the weakness of the flesh and that God strengthens those areas of our life with His Spirit in our new nature. While our struggle is often with the flesh, we also have an adversary who works to steal our abundant life in Christ and diminish our effectiveness in His kingdom.

Satan is the god of this world and master of deception. He has been studying human nature for all time and knows us sometimes better than we know ourselves. He understands our personalities and knows which lies to whisper at just the right time. He searches for the weakness in our flesh and works to put us into his bondage. He believes he can gain control and fights to keep us in darkness. His desire is to distract us so we may never realize who we truly are and the new life we have received. Through his attacks with lies, he finds a foothold in the flesh and influences that area in order to create a stronghold.

A stronghold is any area of our life in which we have believed something that is opposed to the thoughts of God. Often, we believe our experience and circumstances here on earth more than God's promises. These cross-grained beliefs create spiritual obstacles that God desires to destroy. Second Corinthians 10:5 (NIV) says, "We demolish arguments and every pretension that sets itself up against the knowledge of God, and we take captive every thought to make it obedient to Christ." Strongholds are barriers in our relationship and

can disrupt or distort our ability to receive God's love, hear the truth, or experience fellowship with Him. As a result, we cannot see God or ourselves clearly, and we begin to believe things that are not true. Our thoughts become depressed and our spirit downcast. Instead of going to God and allowing Him to reset our thoughts, many seek to keep themselves and their minds busy.

Strongholds cause us to see and perceive the world through a distorted lens. Because we are observing our environment based on incorrect beliefs, we cannot see other people from God's perspective and naturally make unrighteous judgments. Strongholds become the "plank" in our eyes referred to in Matthew 7:3 (NIV), and when we look through this plank at others, all we can see is the "speck" in their eyes. We are unable see the people around us as God sees them, and therefore, judge others to justify ourselves. When we are the recipients of unrighteous judgment, we must call on the power of God to resist temptation. We stand firm in who we are in Christ with quiet confidence. This strength comes from within, and others learn from our example. We supernaturally forgive because we have been forgiven.

Strongholds come from an incomplete or incorrect understanding of the truth. Satan mixes truth with lies to entice us to receive the lies and keep us on the edge of glory. By His death, Jesus destroyed the veil separating believers from the Holy of Holies in the temple when He died on the cross (Matthew 27:51). The Holy of Holies is where God's presence rested on the Ark of the Covenant that contained God's Law in the Old Testament. Christ became the High Priest, and in Him, we now enter into God's presence and commune with Him forever. Satan attempts to build a wall preventing us from experiencing God's presence and fellowship. In a spiritual sense, many Christians remain in the outer court, never going into the temple and experiencing God face to face in the Holy of Holies, now located in our innermost part. We miss out on the communion Christ makes possible for everyone.

A stronghold does not mean we are possessed by a demon. It simply means Satan has a superficial hold on us, and we are controlled by his spirit in that area of our life. Satan can only have influence over the flesh, the part of us that is of the world. In some manuscripts of the Bible, Jesus rebukes his disciples in Luke 9:55 (NKJV) by saying, "You do not know what manner of spirit you are of." Again, in Mark 8:33 (NKJV), Jesus says to Peter, "Get behind Me, Satan! For you are not mindful of the things of God, but the things of men." Truly, Peter's response to the revelation of Jesus's fate, that He was to be brutally murdered, was a natural human reaction. In the flesh, our breath is of the spirit of the world, and we breathe the wrong spirit on the people around us. Jesus recognized this wrong spirit and turned from its influence.

We are no longer of the spirit of this world controlled by Satan but of the Spirit of God. This is a higher spiritual life and our words become laced with a right spirit. By walking in the Spirit, we are no longer mindful of the natural concerns of man, and our mind is stayed on God. John 17:15–17 (NIV) says, "My prayer is not that you take them out of the world but that you protect them from the evil one. They are not of the world, even as I am not of it. Sanctify them by the truth; your word is truth." The Holy Spirit breathes the Word of God into our life, causing our flesh to wither and our true life to spring forth in this world and the next.

When we quiet ourselves in the presence of the Lord and allow His Word to flood our soul, God is able to identify the root of our problem. Our circumstances are just a symptom of the issue, and we must allow God to reveal the lie that feeds unbelief. We must go in to the Father and allow Him to deal with us on a personal level, understanding that while we may struggle with the truth and desire to run or hide, the Father is lovingly massaging our hardened heart. The freedom on the other side is worth the temporary discomfort of nakedness before the Most Holy God. We must make a commitment to walk through the pain with God knowing the struggle is for our good.

When I entered Discipleship School, one of the first exercises Larry had me practice was to quiet myself in the Lord. I had never heard of such a thing, so one night, I went to my bedroom to spend time alone with God. I grabbed a Bible and began to relax. I could sense the Lord was doing something in me, and I wanted to go with Him. He was drawing me into His presence, into the Holy of Holies. I could feel my flesh fighting, and so this took considerable time. Suddenly, I found myself on a beach. I was lying on my belly, and the waves were tossing me upon the sand. A wave began to draw me out to sea, and I reached my arm out to be saved. Just like that, I awoke and was once again in my bedroom.

I was amazed at such a powerful display of God's presence, but I didn't understand what the dream meant. I asked Him and began to relax again. I felt the Father prompt me to go to the Book of James. I opened my Bible and began to read. James 1:6 (NIV) says, "But when you ask, you must believe and not doubt, because the one who doubts is like a wave of the sea, blown and tossed by the wind." God was revealing my doubt.

Doubt creates a divide in our heart. John 11:16 names Thomas Didymus, or the twin, and his name refers to the condition of his heart. When the other disciples came to Thomas and told him they had seen Christ resurrected, Thomas said in John 20:25 (NIV), "Unless I see the nail marks in his hands and put my finger where the nails were, and put my hand into his side, I will not believe." In His love for Thomas, Jesus appeared to him in John 20:27(NIV) and said, "Put your finger here; see my hands. Reach out your hand and put it into my side. Stop doubting and believe." When doubt causes our heart to divide, unbelief hardens the divided parts. We cannot function the way God intended in this condition. In contrast, when Jesus looked upon Nathanael in John 1, He saw a true believer. The Amplified version includes a word that is very helpful in understanding the way God sees us. Jesus said that Nathanael was without duplicity.

While Satan attacks our mind by placing seeds of doubt, he also preys on our emotions. Fear locks the enemy's lies into place. Something unpleasant or abusive has happened; therefore, all future decisions are based on the fear of it happening again. This fear causes us to do and say all sorts of irrational things. Instead of preventing these things from occurring again, fear has a way of inviting them into our life, and strongholds are passed down the generations.

I mentioned Satan found his foothold in my life through my emotions. This foothold allowed the ideas of the world to flood my soul. The world was telling me:

> "You are not safe."
> "She doesn't like you."
> "You are not good enough."
> "You have to be perfect."
> "You are alone."
> "You should be ashamed of yourself."

When we doubt God's word and allow the world's ideas to replace His truth in our heart, we begin to experience a dismal life. We know God forgives, yet we feel shame and guilt. We know God protects, yet we fear for our safety. We say God is sovereign, yet clamor for control of our life.

Sometimes we say we believe, but our emotions and actions tell another story.

After my first child, DJ, was born, fear descended on me like a black cloud. I'm sure hormones left me weakened to the enemy's attacks. I would dread the long, dark nights with my infant. I would fear my son wasn't getting enough to eat, yet was too scared to supplement. He was a fussy baby, and I was afraid I was a bad mom. Guilt gripped me and stifled my joy. Ultimately, I feared for DJ's life. Satan clearly had a hold that kept me earthbound, unable to experience the life Christ had died to give me.

I wasn't free to obey God. I was obsessed with what the experts were saying and tried to obey their advice religiously. I couldn't even trust my own mother's experience. I was miserable, and DJ was miserable too. My fears seemed so real, circumstances seemed to support them, and the world confirmed. Satan also had a stronghold on my husband, and our home was on lockdown; the devil had us under control through fear. At one point, it was as though I could see spiritual chains wrapped around our house.

Shortly after my experience at the women's conference, I was swimming in our neighbor's pond. I wasn't fond of swimming in that pond, but I was preparing for a triathlon, and it was an opportunity to train in "open" waters. I hated the feeling of fish nibbling at my manna-like skin and hated the possibility of a snapping turtle, even though there was no evidence of one living in that pond. I remember the feeling of swimming, water rushing around my body, unable to see what was below. *All right, Lord. I'm swimming in this. Please don't let me sink!* I realized danger would always be present in this world. We feel fear because it is a natural emotion. Jesus knows it by His experience in the flesh. God understands, and that is why His Word consistently encourages us to not be afraid. In Him, we learn to yield this fear to our faith. As for me, I would choose to believe God and trust His will for my life.

Satan capitalizes on our negative experience in this world. God never intended for such abuses to occur. The evil things that happen in life war against faith and wear down hope. We become discouraged in our spirit. Instead of focusing on what is good and right in the world, all we can see is evil and wrong. Our heart has been wounded. Sometimes, these abuses occur with the ones we love most. Someone close may constantly breathe a wrong spirit on us. We begin to believe what we hear with our physical ears more than what the Spirit speaks within. We learn from our experience and agree with the spirit of this world. Through the one that is supposed to love and support us most, we often hear Satan's lies: "You are worthless. You are rejected. You are a disgrace. You are unforgiven."

When guilt and shame become a stronghold, we are living in direct opposition to what is accomplished on the cross. Guilt becomes our filter, and we cannot hear the good in Good News. Even though God's truth is intended to bring relief, all we hear and feel is condemnation, and we are bombarded by Satan's thoughts. God's conviction is gentle and kind, yet when shame is a stronghold, we feel judged instead of released. It is hard to take correction because we hear failure. Perhaps, we feel like we are getting yelled at instead of encouraged. There are many reasons for this, but it could be that we have not yet completely believed in forgiveness. Satan brings up the past to condemn, but if God is bringing up the past, it is for the purpose of healing. We know it is God because He shows us another way. Shame and guilt do not come from the Lord, and we must release them as soon as we feel their sting.

Please know the evil abuses of this world break God's heart. He doesn't turn His back or stand with arms crossed in judgment, ignoring the suffering of the innocent. He is with us, weeping. But this is not the end of the story. He sees this world through victory, and from His perspective, it is finished. For a time, we will suffer just as Jesus suffered. Though our circumstances are different, like Jesus, we suffer pain, rejection, slander, abuse, and abandonment from strangers and loved ones alike. Many times, we suffer at the hands of other Christians and even Christian leaders. Jesus showed us how to endure without sinning (1 Peter 2:21–22). In Him, we overcome the suffering and abuses of the evil one, and He leads us into freedom. God heals our broken heart and protects us from the hardening due to deep, hidden wounds. Do not be discouraged, keep seeking God.

Sometimes, bad habits like procrastination or addiction become Satan's strongholds. Satan loves to take simple pleasures and distort them. The man who enjoys taking a nap increasingly becomes lazy. The woman who enjoys a drink once in a while becomes dependent on alcohol. The teen who loves video games becomes obsessed and can only think about the next time he or she can play. Instead of enjoying the ease of technology and using it for good, the evil one tempts us, and we stumble into sin. Satan uses these harmless things of the world to claim hold on us, and we become progressively controlled by them. They bind us to the earth and become an avenue for Satan's influence in our lives.

Mindsets are another type of stronghold Satan uses to keep us yoked to the temporary. Mindsets are the established set of attitudes held by someone. For example, a person who experiences financial lack, or has a *fear* of financial lack, can take on a belief in poverty. This mindset may lead a person to believe they don't have enough money to tithe, but can tithe their time instead. They may believe spending money is wrong or may spend money like crazy and take on debt. This mindset might lead a person into idolatry of possessions, and this person may unnecessarily feel protective of their belongings.

Competition is another tool that Satan uses as a stronghold to distort our view of God's kingdom. Sadly, competition has created division in God's church. Comparison robs us of joy, and instead of viewing others as members of the same body, we see competing teams. Rather than valuing each ministry, we attempt to put ourselves on top by putting down other churches.

Strongholds often hide behind principles. Satan hijacks certain core beliefs, and entire systems are distorted as a result. We see this in our personal life as well as any human institution from government policy to church doctrine. Living a principled life can be a very honorary way of living; however, it may also become a barrier when the Holy Spirit is guiding us against our human principles. We must be willing to put down our way of thinking and take on the thoughts of God.

It is our identity and calling that disturbs Satan the most. If he can steal our identity, he shuts down our purpose. Time and time again, I see bondage where God's gifts should be manifesting. While there is no way for Satan to know for sure who we are in Christ, he can tell by the way the Spirit of God is moving in our life. He might take the sensitive person and weigh down their emotions or push the ambitious one beyond his or her limits. He edges the bold over the top. Anything Satan can do to destroy the life God has given us, he will do. Notice the way Satan tempted Jesus in the wilderness. In Matthew 4:3 (NLT), Satan said, "If you are the Son of God, tell these stones to become loaves of bread." Next, Satan took Jesus to the highest point of the Temple in Jerusalem and said in verse 6, "If you are the Son of God, jump off!" Satan comes to each one of us and says, "Did God *really* say that?" If he can cause doubt, he has an opportunity to drive a wedge between us and God.

The ultimate temptation for Jesus came when Satan tested His very purpose for being on earth. Matthew 4:8–9 (NLT) says, "Next the devil took him to the peak of a very high mountain and showed him all the kingdoms of the world and their glory. 'I will give it all to you,' he said, 'if you will kneel down and worship me.'" Jesus's purpose was to take authority in heaven and on earth (Matthew 28:18) and destroy the work of the devil in all who believe. God provided the way by the death and resurrection of His Son. Satan no longer has control over us, and Jesus showed us how to respond to his temptations. He quoted Scripture, told Satan to get lost, and Satan had to flee. When Jesus was bombarded by impure thoughts whether by the flesh, through other people, or by Satan himself, He turned and cast it off. We have this same authority in Christ. We are victorious over the flesh, over sin, and over Satan by the power of Jesus Christ through the Holy Spirit.

Near the end of the day at the women's conference, our leaders instructed us to paint over the word we had written on our rock with white paint. During the last session, a smile came over my face as I realized where the exercise was going. They instructed us to write the word "Love" on the painted rock. Immediately, I remembered 1 John 4:18 (ESV), "There is no fear in love, but perfect love casts out fear. For fear has to do with punishment, and whoever fears has not been perfected in love." God cast out my fear and I was genuinely able to receive His love for me and other people. His Spirit flooded my heart and flooded my senses. During our closing time of worship, I looked up at the leader. She looked like an angel, like the most beautiful woman I had ever seen! I could see God's glory in this woman and the sight was breathtaking.

Dear Spirit, tune my ear to hear the sweetness of Your voice, that I may distinguish truth from the fearful, condemning lies of Satan. Help me to discern the spirit of the world and recognize when a message is not from You, that I may turn when the world tempts. May I feel the relief of Your Word, allowing it to bring freedom and life. Help me to see the way out, the way to true life.

Overcoming Idols

There once was a young couple who took a class in order to become financially savvy and get out of debt. They learned wonderful techniques that allowed them to budget their money and still have a little left over for a "slush" fund. They even set aside a tithe to give to the church! After decades of pinching pennies, the couple stored away millions. Their reasoning was simple—be good stewards of the money God had given, save enough for retirement, and leave an inheritance for their children. Enough is relative, so they just kept saving. Little did they know that Satan had been whispering lies that formed a mindset. A thought pattern that was once useful now served to feed greed and drive them to store up more and more money. Instead of being led by God in the way they handled their finances, they simply followed the rules. Every time God prompted them to spend or give their money in a way that didn't make financial sense, they ignored Him. There was no trust or obedience in the way they handled their money. Focus shifted from the giver to the gift and an idol was born.

Perhaps idolatry sounds like an ancient practice that died with golden figurines or something that exists in "less civilized" cultures, but indeed, idolatry is just as rampant today as always. An idol is anything of this world that takes God's position in our heart. It can be anything temporal we believe we need in order to live a happy, successful life. As such, one can readily see that any thought, activity, or object out of balance in our life can become an idol. Instead of seeing the world and all it has to offer as a bonus and a blessing, we believe we need these things in order to survive. Essentially, we say to God, "You are not enough, I need more."

Idols creep in when our priorities become unfocused. These can be very good things and activities, but Satan whispers lies that drive us toward these earthbound objects. We become yoked to temporary pleasures, forsaking the eternal. This can be anything from a house, career, relationship, or even sex. Idols stand in the way of obedience to the Holy Spirit and prevent us from experiencing true satisfaction. It can be very difficult to let go of the things we think we need in order to experience God's best. We have to believe His promises more than what seems to be true in this world.

Strongholds drive us toward idols. Many Christians are unable to see the idols in their lives because their belief system supports them. Idols blind us to God's will. Decisions are based on the premise of the idol, and we are oblivious to the Spirit. What may have once been a pathway to better choices becomes a link to the world and prevents us from experiencing the kingdom of God. Jesus says in Mark 8:34–36 (NLT), "If any of you wants to be my follower, you must turn from your selfish ways, take up your cross, and follow me. If you try to hang on to your life, you will lose it. But if you give up your life for my sake and for the sake of the Good News, you will save it. And what do you benefit if you gain the whole world but lose your own soul?" It is easy to pinpoint idols when talking about material possessions such as cars, money, or clothes, but not as easy to recognize the strongholds that lead us into idolatry. We worship our feelings, ambitions, and passions and may even justify these motivations. The cost of discipleship is total surrender.

We are often called to alter our belief system and let go of our own ideas of a life well-lived in order to follow Christ. There may be traditions, expectations, or plans God is calling us to reconsider in order to do His will. As much as we try, God does not fit within our box of reason. We must remain moldable and open to be influenced by His idea of how our life should be lived. Sometimes, we must release our preconceived notions about who God is and what He requires of us. Many of our beliefs are related to the way we were raised, cultural assumptions, or common practice. We must allow God access into these areas in order to become more like Him in thought and deed.

Money is by far the most difficult thing for human beings to keep in perspective. It is obvious we need money in order to survive, but very difficult for us to believe money comes easily to God. It's hard for even the most devoted Christian to understand how to keep money in proper position within the heart. In Luke 12:13 (NIV), someone from the crowd yelled out to Jesus, "Teacher, tell my brother to divide the inheritance with me." Immediately, Jesus recognized the heart issue and warned the crowd against greed, stating that true life does not come from having an overflow of abundance above and beyond needs. He told a parable in order to teach everyone who was listening. He spoke of a rich man who kept building bigger storehouses to store all his grain, similar to modern families building bigger houses to store all their stuff!

In Luke 12:21, Jesus warned the crowd about those who hoard possessions for themselves, but are poor in relationship with God. This could be someone who continually squirrels away money, but is disobedient with what he or she does with it. Disobedience to the Holy Spirit puts a big damper on our relationship with God, and abundant life becomes a dream, not a reality. In the end, the person who stores up wealth for himself rather than for God is left with nothing of eternal value. Solomon, the richest man in the world, warned this is meaningless.

Jesus continued to instruct his disciples in Luke 12:22 (NLT), "That is why I tell you not to worry about everyday life—whether you have enough food to eat or enough clothes to wear." This advice was profound because Jesus was peeling back the layers of the heart issue. After warning the crowd about greed and piling up riches for oneself, He talked about anxiety and being overly concerned about daily needs. The bottom line is fear. Fear causes the weak in faith to stockpile money and possessions.

God didn't put us on earth, drop us off, and say, "Good luck!" He intended to live with and help us, providing for our every need. With the epidemic of absent fathers in our culture, many don't have a tangible expression of the Father's heart in their life. Others may have grown up with a dad who was physically present but mentally or emotionally absent. We naturally perceive our Heavenly Father to be distant as well, not wanting to talk or commune with us. Deep down, we believe we are on our own to provide for our everyday needs. The burden of responsibility weighs heavily on us. The absence of an earthly father is terribly sad, but not a death sentence. Whatever way our dad may have been deficient can fuel us to seek God as our perfect Father. He Himself fulfills our needs.

In Matthew 11:28–30 (NIV), Jesus said, "Come to me, all you who are weary and burdened, and I will give you rest. Take my yoke upon you and learn from me, for I am gentle and humble in heart, and you will find rest for your souls. For my yoke is easy and my burden is light." Jesus came to take the weight of responsibility if we are willing to give Him control. It is fear that drives us to control our life and money. God's priority is trust and obedience. Jesus says in Luke 12:23 (NIV), "For life is more than food, and the body more than clothes." We need not worry about our fleshly necessities. He knows what we need and will supply it when we trust and obey. Money comes easily to God when He has control!

Jesus then paints a picture of what life with God looks like in Luke 12:24-28. He encourages His disciples to consider how ravens don't store up their food, yet God feeds them every day. They neither sow nor reap, and God takes care of their daily needs. He then describes how God clothes the grass and fields with beautiful lilies. When God is the one providing the riches, our splendor and magnificence is greater than Solomon's!

Jesus gave these examples in order to tear down a stronghold of greed caused by fear. In the flesh, we may be tempted to take Jesus's advice in liberty and say, "Sweet! I don't have to work, I don't have to save, I just need to trust Jesus!" Neither do these verses mean that we have to live from hand to mouth with no savings, nor do they say we have to give away all our possessions and live in poverty. Jesus's illustration is under the assumption of God's control and discipline over our life. In Christ, we need not toil like the rest of the world in order to eat or look good and stylish. God knows and provides, adorning us with His glory. The world frets and worries over such things, but we have another way. The answer lies in verse 31 (NIV), "But seek his kingdom, and these things will be given to you as well."

This is such good news! We don't have to give up nice things in order to avoid greed and please God. The Lord wants to bless us with new cars, a fabulous house, and fashionable clothes. There is no need to hoard these things for ourselves. Our task is to focus on God and His kingdom. When we put our energy toward being united with Christ through submission, we feel rested, comforted, and at ease. He may prompt us to give away our money in one instance, save in another, or spend it on things we want or need. From this perspective, money and possessions become an unnecessary blessing, and we enjoy the things of this world more than most people.

Truly, God wants us to be healthy, happy, and prosperous. It says so in the Bible (Proverbs 28:25–27). It is when pride and greed cloud our vision that God's heart for our material blessing becomes distorted. The flesh informs us we are entitled; the flesh tells us we deserve to be blessed. The flesh is focused on the gift, not the heart and will of the giver. The problem arises when faith is viewed as a transaction. Proper understanding is that God blesses us with spiritual riches that *may* manifest in healing, wealth, and increased possessions. These blessings are "added" (Matthew 6:33 ESV) as a confirmation of God in reality, ever increasing our trust in Him so we will know without a shadow of doubt that He is good and wants good things for us. His focus is eternal, desiring to affirm us so that we are encouraged to hold on to steadfast hope (see Hebrews 6:13–20). He would never add anything He knows would distract us.

God is able to give abundantly when we surrender to His will, but it can be the hardest thing in the world to give up control over the things we have come to idolize. At first, it feels like we are losing. For me, it was my friendships. I have a great appreciation for friends and seek deep, meaningful relationships. In the past, a stronghold of loneliness drove me to seek friendships in an unnatural way with an inexplicable desire for a full-time buddy. I quickly understood I could not expect my husband to fill this role, so I set my sight on the idea of a best friend, which our culture encourages. As I searched for this person, God gently warned me not to seek idols, that what I was looking for was Him. My response was, "Yeah, I know, I know. But I need someone here, this is essential to my happiness." Without realizing it, I was telling God He wasn't enough.

In His love for me, God let me go and allowed me to pursue a friendship with a woman I will call Jenny. We talked daily and I thought she was my everything. For two years, I enjoyed her friendship and enjoyed hanging out with her friends while our children played. Life was perfect, almost. The relationship was riddled with fear of loss and was hard work to maintain. I became confused about my priorities and allowed her to control me, acting to please her instead of God. I had trouble speaking the truth because I was afraid she would be offended. I did all I could to ensure the relationship was unharmed, which actually caused it to become increasingly unhealthy.

The only healthy fear is that which causes us to obey the Lord. There is a holy, reverential fear of the Lord that comes over us and motivates us toward His will. As we obey, our fears are washed away by His love while He floods our heart with wisdom and understanding. Any other kind of fear does nothing but steal, kill, and destroy our abundant life. In other words, Satan uses fear to keep us under his control. When we fear people and what they might think or are overly concerned about pleasing them, we cannot obey the Lord in the way He desires.

Let us consider King Saul in 1 Samuel 15. We have spoken about Saul's disobedience in chapter thirteen when he unlawfully offered a burned offering to the Lord. His disobedience turned to rebellion in chapter fifteen when he took spoils after destroying the city of Amalek. God explicitly told Saul not to spare a thing in the city. When the prophet

Samuel confronted him, he said in 1 Samuel 15:24 (AMP), "I feared the people and obeyed their voice."

There is nothing wrong with wanting to please people or desiring for our loved ones to be happy. But when this desire clouds our judgment and floods out the voice of the Lord, the result is disobedience that leads to rebellion of the heart. We lose ourselves and our identity when people-pleasing becomes a stronghold. We become whoever we believe they want us to be, forsaking our identity in Christ. Instead of boldly obeying the Lord, the fear of people causes us to feel like we are walking on eggshells; we become timid and afraid of offending them. If we continue in this way, we become manipulative, underhanded, and controlling.

The people-pleasing spirit operates under an assumption of happiness. Disappointment is unbearable, so the people-pleaser will stop at nothing to avoid disappointing others. We must allow God to deal with our heart. In Christ, we learn God can use our greatest disappointments to guide us into freedom and His will for our life, leading us into true enjoyment. We learn to deal with our own disappointments through hope. This frees us to trust God, and we are no longer afraid of disappointing others.

God was calling me into closer relationship with Himself, and I could no longer ignore His prompting. He called me to speak the truth in love to Jenny; I couldn't remain silent any longer. I wasn't being honest with her about who I am, so I lovingly shared my heart. To my utter disbelief, she not only hardened her heart to my message but also decided we could no longer be friends. The rejection was crushing.

At the time, it seemed all my fears were coming true. I clamored to take back control, but it was too late. I apologized and hoped she would forgive and forget, but she had already made up her mind. There was nothing I could do but respect her wishes. She was true to her word and did her best to push me out of her life. She forbade our children from playing and made it impossible for my daughter to continue to be a part of her group of friends.

God used the rejection to heal my heart. In my pain, I ran to God. He embraced me and allowed the hard times to purify me. He washed my thoughts with His own, replacing the lies I was believing about myself with the truth. I could see how fear of rejection was motivating my people-pleasing tendencies. I also realized that when fear is my motivation, people aren't really pleased. Nobody likes to be controlled or manipulated, and the people-pleasing spirit tells us we can control their emotions through our actions. I learned for myself that when I obey the Lord, people are truly pleased!

I was forced to confront the stronghold of loneliness that drove me to idolize friendship. Loneliness is a product of the fall and is nothing but a lie in Christ. I realized the homesickness of my early adulthood indicated I wasn't finding my home in Him. I learned what He meant when He said, "I am that friend you are looking for." You see, His Spirit is with us all the time. He's speaking to us regularly, but sometimes, the idols in our life cause His voice to be distorted or even unrecognizable. My desire for a full-time buddy is fulfilled by Him; it doesn't get any better than Him! He wants to laugh with us, have a good time, and love us like no one on earth can. He desires to council us through our hard times and to give us insight and wisdom. He wants to help us in our everyday life by working with us, and we begin to have fun! Through obedience, our sense of His presence becomes more and more acute.

I lived in close proximity to Jenny, so I dealt with the rejection and exclusion on a regular basis. I practiced walking in forgiveness. It was painful to simply drive past her house, and I prayed God would heal my heart, enabling me to extend forgiveness daily. God is a good, good Father. During this time of pain, I was comforted by believing Him. While I grieved the broken friendship, God kept me busy by obeying His Spirit and His presence kept me company. Contentment occupied the empty space in my heart, and the longing for a best friend soon dissipated. My eyes were being opened, and revelation filled me with wonder.

Since then, God has filled my life with many healthy relationships. These relationships are a true blessing because I am not expecting anything from them. Finding contentment in God has freed me to more fully enjoy the people in my life. Old relationships have been enhanced due to my new perspective. God is enough, and if he brings different people in my life for earthly comfort, praise Him! Even my relationship with my husband is deeper than I could have even imagined. In time, God restored the broken relationship with Jenny, though it looks very different than I expected.

We need clear direction from the Lord regarding our relationships. We must allow Him to clarify His purpose in bringing certain people into our life. The Lord brings some to influence us, and some we are called to influence. If we don't confuse the two, we will understand our relationships from His perspective, and many of our fears will naturally ease.

The key is to put down our agenda and our idols and listen with the intention of submitting. If we obey His voice, our lives will rise above our earthly condition—this existence that is riddled by the consequence of sin. Jesus took sin and saved us from its burden. Jesus tore down the veil between heaven and earth. Our lives can be the recipient and the conduit for God's kingdom here and now.

Dear Father, please open my eyes to the way Satan has deceived me and led me to fill a need with things of this world. Please reveal my heart condition. Allow me to see my struggles as an opportunity to come to You and know You better.

Chapter 9

Awakening

I didn't grow up in a tradition that necessarily taught me to be listening for what we describe as the voice of the Holy Spirit. I remember exercises designed to find a quiet place to be with the Lord, but usually, that meant reading my Bible and learning more information about God. When I entered the Discipleship School, Larry spoke God's Word over me and into my life. For the first time, I could recognize God's tender voice without looking at the words in my Bible. Something clicked.

I realized God had been speaking to me all along—that I could and indeed did hear His voice. I had become familiar with His character and understood His purpose through my Bible reading. I began to register His voice and recognize His Spirit in words that were spoken out loud. I could hear God's power and authority in the message and was aware when He was speaking to me. Through Larry's example, I felt I had been given permission to believe the still, small voice in my spirit and the floodgates opened.

I went into a time of deep purification, which was a very intense period. It seemed as though I was in a refining fire, and God was purifying my faith by drawing off the impurities. Proverbs 25:4 (ESV) says, "Take away the dross from the silver, and the smith has material for a vessel." For about a month, it was like a switch had been turned on, and God's voice was a steady stream. It was as though thirty years of thoughts were being rewritten, while every new thought was captured and submitted in obedience to Christ. God was teaching me how He thinks. In everything I did, God was telling me His perspective. Many strongholds were being loosened in my mind as I received God's thoughts without doubt. While this time was challenging because many of my beliefs were contrary to the thoughts of God, I allowed Him to lovingly correct me. I knew God's correction was good news and no longer felt condemned for my waywardness.

It was as though God was saying, "Finally! Let's go, girl!" He had my undivided attention and was working to quicken my soul; God was stirring my whole being alive. Truly, I had been given new life many years ago, so this was a time of reviving as the Lord was bringing this new life to the surface. I was experiencing the thoughts and *feelings* of new birth.

In so many ways, I felt as though I was being harvested; I had a sense of my soul being awakened, allowing me to perceive new life in Christ. In Matthew 13:24–30, Jesus tells a parable about a man who sowed good wheat seed. While his servants were sleeping, his enemy came and sowed weeds that looked similar to wheat. For the time, the man left the weeds to grow so as to not disrupt the growing wheat. But come harvest time, the weeds were bound and thrown into the fire. From a spiritual perspective, this is what was happening. I was awakening from a spiritual slumber and was being harvested for the kingdom of God, and the lies Satan had planted were bound and cast out. I was free to trust and obey God.

Regeneration is said to be a secret act of God. When we receive the Gospel, He causes our spirit to be born (again) of the Spirit of God. He opens our mind to discern spiritual realities and frees our enslaved will to obey God. Jesus said we cannot see the kingdom of God unless we are born again. He awakens our senses to perceive His kingdom on earth as it is in heaven. He is the One who imparts new spiritual life in our innermost being, and He is the One who influences our mind to confess belief. Ezekiel records this revelation in Ezekiel 36:26 (NASB), "Moreover, I will give you a new heart and put a new spirit within you; and I will remove the heart of stone from your flesh and give you a heart of flesh." The only secret is this new spirit exists whether we realize it or not. God renews a right spirit within, and we are born of God. He removes our hardened heart and gives us a soft, obedient heart. God is revealing His miraculous work deep within our spirit. We experience our new flesh even before God gives us a new body in the next age. This flesh is tempered by the Spirit and is Christlike.

Ezekiel doesn't stop there. He gives us a beautiful picture of the complete work of God. He writes in verse 27, "I will put My Spirit within you and cause you to walk in My statutes, and you will be careful to observe My ordinances." Regeneration affects the whole person. What starts in our inner spirit infiltrates our mind, will, and emotions and then spills out into reality through our works. His Spirit *causes* us to obey God's will, His purpose, and the law written on our heart. This is such good news! It is not our will or good effort that causes change, but the will of God through the Holy Spirit in our life. This should be a great relief to every Christian, but many have not yet realized the Spirit's power in their life. It is not left up to us to toil and work to create evidence of salvation. It's God's job to produce fruit in our life.

Furthermore, Ezekiel writes about the result of God's spiritual work in the land. He writes in verses 29–30 (AMP), "I will also save you from all your uncleanness, and I will call forth the grain and make it abundant and lay no famine on you. And I will multiply the fruit of the tree and the increase of the field, that you may no more suffer the reproach and disgrace of famine among the nations." Words like abundant, multiply, and increase are all used in connection with the kingdom of heaven. We have an opportunity, even obligation, to live like God's promises are true! We walk into the reality of His promises by faith. Heaven is manifested on earth through our faithfulness.

This kind of faith is seen throughout the Bible. The truly faithful lived like God's promises were already true. Samson and Abraham seem to have been operating under the new covenant even before Jesus came in reality here on earth. They lived according to the promptings of the Spirit and walked in obedience to the law written on their heart. Jeremiah 31:33 (ESV) wrote, "I will put my law within them, and I will write it on their hearts." Truly, this was a promise at the time; the earth had not yet seen the fulfillment since they were under the old covenant or under the authority of the Law of Moses. When Christ came, died, and rose again, these promises written by the prophets went into effect through a new covenant. The door has been opened for all to experience intimacy with God and to be led and empowered by the Holy Spirit. We cannot read the stories in the Bible and distance ourselves from the characters. We are just as special to God as they are, capable of great faith and extraordinary experiences.

In order to become aware of regeneration and the abundant life, we must allow God to reveal His law. The Bible is

God's testimony to all man. The church is the manifestation of Christ. The Holy Spirit is our intimate connection to God. So many desire relief from the effects of sin but are unwilling to do the will of God. We cling to quick fixes, hanging on to the temporary, and are unwilling to make the commitment to the eternal. We are distracted by the demands of this world and our life. We struggle to give up what we see and experience here on earth and are unable to grasp God's spiritual realities. Our heads are down and we are busy with the task at hand. God is saying, "Look up!" He wants to release us from the worries of daily life, to trust Him, in order to free us to dwell on eternal things.

A young Martin Luther struggled with the righteousness of God. He read in the Bible that the righteous would live by faith, but he didn't believe he was righteous. He wrestled deeply until it finally clicked that faith is a gift of God. At that moment, he realized his holiness had nothing to do with his own striving but was completely and utterly a work of God through His gift. With this new understanding, Martin put his trust in Jesus and said, "Here I felt as if I were entirely born again and had entered paradise itself through gates that had been flung open. The whole of Scripture gained a new meaning. And from that point on the phrase the 'justice of God' no longer filled me with hatred, but rather became unspeakably sweet by virtue of a great love."

During this time of awakening, I once again needed to face the reality that God had called me His prophetess. I was reminded of a vision, or picture in my imagination, that God had given me as a young lady when I was trying to decide what to do after graduation from high school. I saw myself on a path lined with crowds of people. I was following behind a leader who was proclaiming the gospel. I was collecting and tending to the people in the wake of the leader. Recalling this vision, I finally realized why I struggled so much in college.

I had ignored a calling into ministry in order to pursue engineering. Going into ministry didn't make any sense to me at that time, so I chose what did, thereby choosing my own way in what I thought was right.

I desired more information about the prophetic calling, and the Lord provided. I began reading Larry's insight and explanation of the role of the prophet. I found everything in my spirit saying, "Yes!" I was intimately connected to his words and experiences. Through this lens, all the seemingly random fragments of my life, past and present, suddenly fell in line and made perfect sense. It was as though I had been viewing life through a frayed metal pipe, and God caused the metal pieces to lay into place so I could see the light at the end of the tunnel. Confusion melted into understanding and I felt peace. God was confirming His Word in me, my soul was being stirred to life, and it was an exciting time. However, the weight of this divine calling quickly dampened the excitement. I knew I needed to accept this mantle in order to experience fulfillment of God's life and purpose, but at what cost? This role was not to be mishandled; it was His way, or no way. Who was I to take on this role?

That Sunday at church, our pastor spoke about taking off the old and putting on the new. Ephesians 4:22–24 (NLT) says, "Throw off your old sinful nature and your former way of life, which is corrupted by lust and deception. Instead, let the Spirit renew your thoughts and attitudes. Put on your new nature, created to be like God—truly righteous and holy." In order to illustrate this truth, our pastor took off a dark jacket and put on a white one. In the Spirit, I could see the Lord handing me a shining, brilliantly white coat, and I needed to put it on. I couldn't keep one arm in the dark jacket and put the other in the white coat. The prophetic mantle is included in my new nature. God was urging me to go "all in."

Our worship leader started singing the closing song, "The Stand," by Hillsong United. The lyrics say, "I stand, with arms high and heart abandoned. . . My soul Lord to you surrendered." My arms remained crossed. "Lord, I can't! I can't! I can't. . ." I screamed inside. Suddenly, my arms fell limp. With tears streaming down my cheeks, I surrendered to God's calling on my life.

First and foremost, prophets are called to point others to God's heart and the redemptive work of Jesus Christ. We are trained in the spirit realm to hear and communicate the spoken and written Word of God full-time, no matter what we are doing or who we are with. The reason God has sharpened my spiritual hearing, talking to me so frequently, is because He has called me to function in the role of prophet within the body of Christ, teaching and equipping others according to God's purpose for their life.

Whether we have a calling into ministry or not, God has poured out His gifts on all His children by the presence of His Spirit. Some may primarily discern His will through hearing His voice, and some may feel His Spirit and simply have an impression of the right way. Still others may have a heightened sense of sight, and use their spiritual sight to see the correct path. We all have been given the ability to obey in an intimate way, and each have a personal calling in the body of Christ. I help facilitate growth through bringing these callings into the light, so others may know and operate in their true identity. He gives me the ability to recognize who He created His servants to be, and I confirm that person by treating them accordingly. I see that which exists in the spirit realm, calling forth what has already been released in the spirit of the believer according to the purpose of God.

It may be tempting to believe those who are called into the ministry of the gospel are somehow more special to God, but this is not the case at all. Whether we are called to lead or support leaders in their role within the church, we are all critical to God's mission on earth to establish His eternal kingdom. As humans, we see a vertical hierarchy of authority; however, in God's kingdom, we are all His children. From His perspective, authority is lateral—the same body, different functions. In 1 Corinthians 12, Paul relates the church to the parts of the body, confirming the absolute necessity of every part and giving greater honor to the seemingly weaker or hidden parts. It is natural to see the body standing up, elevating church leaders far above ourselves. But the truth is that the body is lying down, prostrate in front of God's holy throne. If we can get beyond our own pride, we see how this body works in extraordinary ways when we value each part equally. We all submit to Jesus as the head, and if we don't fight Him for control, we work, grow, and flow as He intends.

The spirit of prophecy has been released to all believers through the Holy Spirit, and I simply function as a forerunner, calling forth this gift in His body. We all have been given the gift to hear and respond to His voice. The Lord is training me to equip others to fulfill God's calling on their lives, building up the body of Christ until all oneness of faith is established on earth. Until the unity of faith is established, until the body flows as one in God's Spirit, until the body has fully matured, the prophets will speak and call people back to His heart and purposes (Ephesians 4:11–13). God is raising a new generation of prophets to speak forth His Word into existence.

Prophets are also God's seers. He gives us the ability to see spiritual things that are not seen by the natural eye; we see by the Spirit's power, again, a gift that is poured out for all. When God opened my eyes, I could see the Spirit's work in and around people. I could see things that actually existed in the spiritual realm. In this way, I was given the ability to guide people closer to God's heart, calling out any stumbling blocks and pointing them to Jesus. I embraced my role as an encourager, supporting and drawing out the things of God in other people. I was able to recognize that which was from God and worked to nurture those things.

In addition to seeing the things of God, I could also identify those things that were not of His Spirit. This is the spiritual gift of discernment. One morning, a woman I knew became especially vocal in church. I didn't think anything of it because she was saying things in support of our pastor. But as it continued, I realized the spirit I was hearing was not of God. The woman had been mentally ill, and this spirit was using her weakness to distract others and mock God.

Immediately, I bowed my head, and God instructed me to pray. I didn't understand what was happening, but the Spirit lead me to bind the spirit; it could no longer make any other utterances. The woman began to quiet down. As our pastor was wrapping up, he instructed us to bow our heads and not get up or move around. God's power came strongly on me and was leading me to lay my hand on the woman. I resisted for a moment, but His power was so strong I felt as though I would die if I did not obey the Lord. Instinctively, I slipped off my shoes and silently crossed the isle to where she was sitting. I had no idea what I was doing, but I kneeled and placed my hand on her back. I became a conduit and God's power moved through me into this woman. She shot straight out of her seat and then crumbled over the seat in front of her. I want to be clear. This woman was a Christian and was not possessed by a demon. However, just as the Spirit of God can use man as a mouthpiece, so Satan can influence our words by the flesh. This spirit had no right or claim to this woman, and I was easily able to throw it off by the authority given me in Christ. We all possess this authority.

As a prophet, I can see and hear the spiritual realm as one with physical reality. We would call these manifestations. Just as God was made manifest in Jesus, so also our enemy can manifest himself through people. One night we were at church, and as the closing song began, a guest started running down the aisle. The woman took a lap around the auditorium. That in and of itself was very strange for our church, but what I saw and heard was even more alarming. Though the band was playing, I could hear distinct footsteps that echoed unnaturally. When I looked, the woman was crouched over, arms extended straight behind her, and I heard a soft, gliding noise. In the middle of the song, the woman began screaming in the back of the room. What I heard was screeching that made my blood run cold. *Lord, I'm scared,* I thought. Just then, the music began to swell in a way I had never experienced, and I could sense God's power pulsing in the crescendo. Soon, the woman could no longer be heard and was silenced. After the song, a movement caught my eye in the corner of the auditorium. As the pastor closed the service, this woman was cowering against the wall, arms and hands tucked in against her chest. It was an incredible display of God's power over the enemy, and I was reminded to not fear the devil's antics.

I share these stories not to sensationalize the spirit realm, but to communicate the reality of its existence. My desire is to confirm what is written in the Bible. Angels and demons are just as real as what we see explained by the Prophets of old. This need not scare anyone because by the authority of Christ in us, the enemy is defeated.

A true spiritual awakening is when the Holy Spirit opens our senses to a new reality. We are a completely new person with a heart capable of pleasing and obeying God. We are focused on Christ who redeems, the Spirit who empowers, and the kingdom of God to which we now belong. This becomes our reality and experience now and for eternity. This is really good news!

When Christ came to earth, spiritual principle became physical reality. Every truth revealed by the Prophets was manifest in Jesus. To the man born blind in John 9, spiritual rebirth occurred with physical sight. This illustrated the truth expressed by so many in the faith, from the Psalmist to John Newton who wrote, "I once was lost but now am found, was blind but now I see." We are awakened to His Spirit moving in our everyday lives. We see His hand of provision, perceive His ways, and discern His will. We sense God's presence and follow His leading into the abundant life. This new reality is available to all who hear and respond to God's call.

Father, stir my heart and mind. Awaken me to spiritual realities, draw me into Your good, and perfect will. Open my eyes to see Your Spirit, open my ears to hear your Word, and increase my sensitivity to feel Your presence. I want to taste and smell Your goodness in my life. Father, I want more of your kingdom reality in my everyday life. Please reveal these things.

Chapter 10

God's Glory

Several years ago, I asked God to show me His glory. I figured if Moses did it, so could I! I don't think I understood what I was asking. I thought I was asking for a vision, a picture, or a dream of His presence. I thought I was praying for an experience that would sharpen my *sense* of Him, a sort of spiritual tuning if you will. God's glory is so much more. God's glory is the manifestation of His full character—all that He is. God's glory is heavenly reality breaking into the reality of our world in miraculous ways. It is the open display of His greatness and power so all men can see and know *I Am*.

Just as God covered Moses with His hand, no man can fully see God's glory and live. So we receive glimpses of what we can handle. Never would I have guessed what God had in mind for our family. We were living on the fourteen wooded acres at the time. There was nothing to be seen but trees upon trees and perhaps an occasional black Angus cow at the farm next door. One summer afternoon, I picked the children and their friend up from camp and brought them home. I sent the kids outside as I prepared dinner. Suddenly,

DJ came to me in hysterics. He tended to be a bit dramatic, so I quickly tried to defuse the situation. I calmly asked him what was wrong and steadily went for my shoes.

"No! You must hurry!" he yelled. "A tree fell on Holly!"

Trying not to panic, I found my boots and started out to the back woods. As I began the trek down the path, I could see our son's friend guiding Holly, my nine-year-old daughter, toward the house. I broke into a run. Her nose was clearly broken as a large, dark bubble was forming on the side. I braced her feeble body and she weakly said, "Mom, it hurts so bad." You know it's bad when a child doesn't have the energy to cry.

I brought her back to the house and laid her on the floor. The boys raced to find a pillow and did all they could to comfort her. I called my husband and told him Holly was badly injured. I thought I should go to the county hospital to get her nose x-rayed. The boys and I gingerly laid Holly on the floor of our minivan, complete with blankets and pillows. I remember feeling concerned about the blood choking her and giving her some ibuprofen for pain.

Holly had found a partially broken tree and was swinging on it like a gymnastics bar. When she swung, the trunk broke loose and fell on her face. DJ and his friend, both age eleven, rushed to her side and lifted the tree enough for her to scoot out from underneath. Thankfully, she lost consciousness for just a moment. I called the friend's mom and informed her a small tree had fallen on Holly's head, and let her know her son was waiting at our house with my boys. Later, she told me my voice was monotone like a robot. There was no emotion, no inflection in my words, only information.

Twenty-five long minutes later, we arrived at the emergency room. Holly was silent the entire ride. I went to the back of the van to get her; to my horror, her whole face was swelling and her eyes were filling with blood. I braced her little body, and we walked through the doors. The moment seemed to last forever as the receptionist looked at Holly and I looked at the receptionist. I was in shock. Finally, I muttered, "A tree fell on her head." That is when I realized we were at the wrong place. Our county hospital was not set up for severe trauma.

After what felt like an eternity (but really was just a few seconds), the nurse grabbed a wheelchair and wheeled Holly back to a room. Life was moving in slow motion. I rested a moment against the wall outside the room and just breathed. It was a whirlwind as nurses rushed around, not exactly sure how to handle the situation. Unexpectedly, one snapped a picture on her phone and whipped it around to show Holly. *Wait, why was that necessary?*

All at once, the swirl of activity left the room. Alone together, Holly looked at me and asked, "How is this all going to heal?" Without skipping a beat, I looked my little girl straight in the eyes and said, "Perfectly."

The doctor came in and announced they would be taking Holly for a CT scan. There was more rushing, and Holly was gone. *Oh my God!* I realized, *Her brain could be bleeding!* I heard God's calming voice say, "Her brain is fine, but she will go to Cincinnati for surgery."

I don't remember much of what the doctor said except that his words were strangely a relief. I could hear that Holly was going to be alright. They prepped her for an IV filled with morphine, and we were to be transported by ambulance to Cincinnati Children's Hospital. Getting the IV inserted was difficult, and the trip by ambulance was simply dreadful during rush hour; but the moment we hit the doors in Cincinnati, we were in excellent hands. One by one, the medical specialists came to say Holly would be fine. All of them cleared Holly to leave the hospital. God was assuring me she was going to be okay.

By this time, Holly didn't even look human. She looked like pictures I had seen of patients after plastic surgery, faces unrecognizable because they were so grossly swollen and bandaged. This is what Casey walked in to see.

"Aww. . .," he said tenderly as he entered the room and was filled with compassion for his daughter. Not a soul could control their emotion when they walked in and saw her condition.

Trauma is like a thick veil of emotion; it is as though you can't even see your foot right in front of you. I was like a child, not able to fully process the circumstances or see the next step. I just wanted to go home as if everything would be fine. It was somewhere around three in the morning when there was controversy about whether Holly should be released. Finally, around 4:00 a.m., we were led to our room. Holly was to be admitted for observation.

Longing for it all to be over, we were disappointed. But as I watched the next forty-eight hours unfold, I believe it was God's protection and assurance that allowed us to remain under the skilled care of medical professionals. In these circumstances, plastic surgeons must wait for the swelling to decrease before repairing the damage. Many of Holly's facial bones had been crushed. A combination of swelling with sharp bone fragments introduced the risk of piercing the brain fluid, which could lead to a dangerous infection.

Holly slept the entire day after the accident. I was so consumed by what I saw on the outside, I wasn't able to fully understand what was happening on the inside. I was unable to discern that she slept because she sustained a traumatic brain injury. During my down time at the hospital, I called my friend and sobbed. All I could say was, "Holly's fine," until I could compose myself to tell her what happened. After the conversation and prayer, I returned to Holly's room. I sat quietly in the darkened room when a rush of supernatural peace washed over me. Something was happening. I checked my Facebook page, and my friend had posted an urgent prayer request that quickly was shared all over the nation! I can only imagine how many people were praying. Later, I found out entire church groups had been praying. Ministering angels came to relieve my distress.

The second night Casey stayed at the hospital, and I went to his parents' house where our boys were staying. I spent a few moments with each child as I put them to bed. Our oldest, DJ, said that he had read my texts from the day. I was concerned because I had sent sensitive information to his grandparents about Holly's status. I was afraid it would have scared him.

"Mom," he said as he looked at me intently, "Holly could have died."

"This is true," I responded.

As I watched his face, I could see this realization did not scare him or even make him sad. What I saw in my son's face was thanksgiving and peace. He knew Holly could have died, but he also knew God saved her and that she was going to be okay. He went to bed encouraged. I wanted to go to bed encouraged! I saw DJ's faith and it inspired me. That night while sleep eluded me, I cried out to God. I could see the disciples in the boat while the storm raged (Matthew 8:23–27). I could see the panic as they woke Jesus from His sleep and wanted Him to calm the storm.

"My child," God said to me, "You humans want me to calm the storm, but I want you to walk on water." I could see Peter getting out of the boat and making his first steps toward Jesus (Matthew 14:22–29).

"Father," I bowed my head in submission, "I want to walk on water. Please show me how."

Holly's road to healing was a long and winding path. Her care at the hospital shifted dramatically as each expert came and gave their perspective. At one point, the Lord spoke the word, "jibe." I remembered from lessons as a child that jibing is a sailing technique in which a "zigzag" pattern is used to sail downwind. Many sailboats are significantly faster using this technique, and it can be safer than running straight downwind. Although the path may seem longer from the vessel's perspective, the increased speed compensates for the extra distance. Armed with this insight, my husband Casey and I were prepared to trust God's care through the team of doctors at Cincinnati Children's Hospital. The Lord was teaching me to relax and watch Him direct Holly's healing.

This insight helped us trust God the day of Holly's plastic surgery. We had previously met with one surgeon who explained how she would reconstruct Holly's shattered nose, insert a wire, and use metal plates to hold the external bones of her face together. A few days after that consultation, we received a call informing us the surgery had been moved to the main hospital campus and a different surgeon would be completing the work. While this was a big change, I trusted it was God's plan. What we didn't expect was a completely different surgical approach. There was no time to question this new strategy; we were in God's hands and decided to trust the surgeon God had chosen for Holly.

In the months following the accident, God allowed me to see childlike faith in action. I watched and was encouraged as Holly walked through trauma into whole healing. I could see her releasing spiritual burdens that we as adults tend to hold on to and carry. I witnessed how she passed through pain, fear, and many other emotions, letting go of all things temporal.

When we brought Holly home from the hospital, our youngest son couldn't even look at her. He snapped his head around and wrapped his arms tightly around Grandma's neck. Holly experienced nightmares, uncharacteristic behaviors, and feelings of depression. There were difficult conversations as I pointed her to God, finding her value and beauty in Christ. Jesus calmed my emotions by allowing me to see Holly wasn't staying in those dark places, but walking to freedom on the other side. In those moments of faith, I could see her healing, inside and out, would be complete by God's power.

One day, Holly woke up from a nap crying. I wasn't sure what was going on and ran for the prescribed pain medication. By the time I reached her, she was sobbing. I tried to give her the medication and water. In between sobs she said, "Mommy, why are you giving me these?"

I said, "Aren't you in pain?" I was bewildered by the sudden outburst of emotion. We were scheduled to make one of our very first outings. She was courageously going to spend time with her girlfriend, despite her "scary" looks. Not sure what to do, I helped Holly into our van. By that time, she was wailing. I called her friend's mom and told her we wouldn't be able to make it. I'm sure she could hear Holly wailing in the background. *Lord, what do I do?* I decided distraction was the best method and just started driving. We ended up at her friend's house. I ran to the door, Holly still crying in the van.

With wide eyes and a look like a deer in headlights, I exclaimed, "She's melting down!" Holly's sweet friend, appropriately named Grace, quietly went to the van door and simply stood by her side. Within minutes, Holly got out of the van and followed Grace into the house. Relieved, I sat with my friend, Grace's mother, and we chatted outside. She graciously invited us to stay for dinner. In those moments, I could feel God loving on us and sending the comfort we needed at the exact moment we needed it most. We were not alone.

Sure enough, the outside healing was perfect. We had an exceptional surgeon who did amazing work. Six weeks after the accident, I held a picture up to Holly and confirmed, aside from residual bruising, she looked exactly the same! This was stunning knowing she was unrecognizable after the accident. Two years later, her first x-ray was taken for orthodontic purposes. The orthodontist confirmed the plastic surgeon had indeed performed a phenomenal job. Today, there is no external trace a tree ever fell on her head!

Using ordinary doctors and hospitals, God caused us to walk in an extraordinary way. With faith and hope, we were able to navigate a life-threatening situation with relative ease. When fear crept in and Satan filled my mind with "what-ifs," I was able to recall God's personal Word and affirm my trust in Him. More than once, I was tempted to worry and use the circumstances to support my fears. However, God had spoken directly to the situation and His Word settled the issue. I chose to believe Him in those moments of fear.

Through trust and obedience, the Lord taught me what it means for a Christian to "walk on water." While our circumstances may be subject to the fallen nature of the world, God empowers His children to walk above the common pitfalls and valleys of the natural man. A child who experiences severe trauma or loss often carries emotional baggage for the rest of their life. The stress of the experience alone can cause developmental challenges or delays. Because of this, many parents fear for their children, driving them to control their life in an attempt to avoid pain and suffering. The extraordinary reality is that God enables His children to walk through trauma without being traumatized for life.

I have to admit, it was hard to believe Holly's brain was "fine" those first few months after the accident. She would start tasks and not complete them. She would show unusual lack of self-control with her brothers. I wondered if this is a normal kid behavior or the result of a head injury. I was tempted to run ahead of God and take control of the situation. However, I remembered the rest of Peter's story in Matthew 14:30–31 (NIV). "But when he saw the wind, he was afraid and, beginning to sink, cried out, 'Lord, save me!' Immediately Jesus reached out his hand and caught him. 'You of little faith,' he said, 'why did you doubt?'"

The reality is her bones were shattered like eggshells to the base of the brain, and her brain was badly bruised. While the plastic surgeons pieced together the outside bones, there was nothing they could do on the inside. The neuroscience team warned us Holly might struggle in school. I clung to God's promise that her brain was fine. We waited for this promise to be fulfilled.

God speaks from a timeless position, and when He speaks, it is eternal truth. From His perspective, Holly was already healed. I chose to believe Him and live as though His promise was true, even when the circumstances seemed to suggest otherwise. When we walk through trials with God, He lifts our despair and gives us hope.

During fall conferences at school, we met with Holly's math teacher, and she mentioned her desire to accelerate Holly. Quite frankly, we laughed it off. Holly had always been a good and disciplined student, but we knew math just wasn't her language. In the past, she complained about math being too hard and believed she wasn't good at it. I began to notice math was coming more naturally, and I even mentioned it to her. She confirmed it was easy "all of a sudden."

Later in the school year, we received a letter in the mail explaining that as a result of Holly's testing, the state of Ohio had identified her as gifted in math. This was incredible! I believe the results were tangible proof that God had supernaturally healed her brain and the jump in test scores was simply a by-product of being touched by the miraculous hand of God. The positive differences in school didn't stop there. Before the accident, Holly had lagged in reading comprehension, making reading a chore she didn't enjoy. She had reading goals at school that she frequently did not reach before the accident. She soared above her goals the following year. I believe her comprehension had been enriched by God's power.

People want to know why God would allow pain and suffering, especially in the case of our children. When we align our thoughts with His thoughts, we see for ourselves that God is good. God's heart is love, salvation, redemption, and restoration. Because His focus is eternal, He allows suffering even to the point of death on a cross. In His love for us, He allows whatever is necessary to be with us now and forever.

The disciples asked similar questions when Jesus was on earth. They asked Him why a man was born blind, even wondering if it was due to his sin. Jesus answered in John 9:3 (NIV), "'Neither this man nor his parents sinned,' said Jesus, 'but this happened so that the works of God might be displayed in him.'" Jesus then miraculously healed the blind man.

There are plenty of testimonies of modern miracles, of His power manifesting on earth. By the presence of the Holy Spirit, we possess this power as He appropriates the gifts of healings and miracles according to His will. Our Perspective allows us to recognize and experience this power. It is hard to understand why He doesn't instantly and divinely fix problems more often, especially in our personal situation. We are tempted to believe He is distant and doesn't care about the details of our life. We pull up our bootstraps and trudge through the mess in our own power. But God is sovereign and doesn't give us what we think is best, because He knows what is best. He wants to teach us to walk with Him through the brokenness of this world. He wants to show us how to take care of ourselves in a way that glorifies Him, learning to depend on Him for strength. Ultimately, He knows what is best according to His eternal plan, and His focus is always on releasing faith, building trust, and producing the fruit of righteousness in His children.

I remember the day our family doctor examined Holly's CT scan. He quietly closed his laptop and solemnly remarked, "She's a lucky girl." A neighbor commented, "She's too lucky." After describing the accident to a different neighbor, she exclaimed how she could "see" God's hand covering Holly's face, protecting her precious organs inside.

It doesn't take a spiritual person to recognize divine intervention on Holly's behalf. Manifestations of the Spirit through signs and wonders are a natural part of life in Christ. We cannot deny the extraordinary reality of miracles. God is looking for a willing vessel for His kingdom realities to break through into the reality of this world. It makes sense He would choose a lowly child to manifest His power and greatness. All men can see God's glory through the miracle of Holly's salvation, healing, and deliverance here on earth.

Lord, I believe you work in supernatural ways here on earth. You have given me faith; help my unbelief. I trust You to manifest in my life through divine intervention, miracles, and physical healing. Open my eyes to see the wonders of Your love each and every day. Teach me to expect miracles.

Chapter 11

New Nature

If I wanted to describe my first-born son using one word, it would be intense. I am convinced DJ wasn't planning on coming out of the womb the day he was born. I joke that he got too big, accidentally broke my water, and held out his arms and legs in an "X" position to prevent birth. Sixteen hours later, we decided it would be good if the doctors induced labor, and another eight hours later, he was born.

DJ seemed to have an idea of how life should go from the beginning, but as his mom, I didn't get the memo. Those first few years were pretty intense for mother and son. I remember one time, Casey and I tried to go out on a date. I handed DJ over to my mother-in-law, and he arched his little back and released the biggest wail a baby could possibly muster. I looked at her and said, "I think he might be strong-willed."

She smiled a knowing smile and said, "I think so."

It also became clear early on that DJ was very intelligent. Observant people noticed, even as a baby, his mind was constantly working. As he grew, it became obvious his gift made him very precocious, and Mom had a big task.

He'd move so fast and make such big messes that I struggled to keep up. I felt like I had twins. Before I could clean one mess, another had already been made. I remember my loving mother-in-law giving me much-needed advice, "You need to stay one step ahead of him." I thought, *How do I stay ahead if I don't know where he is going?*

It was also evident my strong-willed, intelligent baby was intensely sensitive. He had a milk allergy that I believe caused him discomfort, making him more irritable than most babies. It was challenging to get through the day without a major meltdown. I would organize my grocery list in order and race through the store before he'd had enough. Thankfully, when he was two, I had a friend who also had a strong-willed two-year-old, and we would drop our precocious children at each other's house in order to get the groceries done! Frequently, he would get so upset that he'd tantrum until he threw up. When he was a baby, we used to set a swing outside, an activity he enjoyed, just to take a few minutes to eat dinner in peace. Before he even learned to speak, he was bossing me around as I tried my best to appease my baby.

While DJ's gifts made him difficult to raise, I could see glimpses of incredible ability, passion, and awareness. He never took information at face value. He was constantly seeking to understand what was happening under the surface. The "why" stage was particularly interesting, and DJ would stop at nothing until I gave up and said, "Because that's the way God made it." Thank goodness that was an acceptable answer! He would baffle me with his questions that revealed what he was thinking about. When Google came along, I was relieved to be able to say, "I don't know, DJ. Google it." His sensitivity brought amazing intuition, and as a child, I noticed he could perceive things most people didn't notice. I would watch my young son gently work to cheer up a cranky, old man and make him smile. He would pick up on the emotions of people around him and respond accordingly. He sensed things in his environment and seemed to see below the surface of people and circumstances.

I chose to see his strong will as a gift. I knew if we could train him in the way he should go early on, he would walk the straight and narrow for life. Family history proved it was possible. With my dominant tendencies, I thought the way was to simply demand immediate obedience. I perceived his strong will as rebellion. The constant friction between us was unbearable, and I was exhausted every night. I grew to be angry all the time, which was uncharacteristic for me. One day, I asked the Lord why I was so angry. He said, "It is because you are afraid."

I believe DJ was especially affected by the stronghold of fear during those early years. Looking back, I can see the effects of the spirit of fear in DJ's life. The tantrums increased, bed-wetting persisted, and night terrors developed; and eventually, he began to throw up in his sleep. He was extraordinarily sensitive to stress, good or bad, and had negative reactions after particularly exciting days. We needed to be very careful about his sleep routine, making sure he got enough and stayed on schedule. When he was four, I dropped to my knees. Something had to change! He was just a little boy, so I prayed, "Lord, change me."

I prayed God would make me the mother DJ needed and began to put aside my preconceived notions of a good parent. I started thinking more about the parent God wanted me to be and less about what other people thought. As I let go of pride, the embarrassment melted away. I was more interested in being an effective mother for DJ than looking like the perfect mom to other people. Since my mother-in-law survived raising her own strong-willed son, my husband, I learned from her way with DJ. I watched her lovingly meet his needs in the way he needed. She understood and didn't judge him. I noticed she would redirect him before a conflict even occurred. I wondered if that was what she meant about being one step ahead.

I became a child while God taught me about Himself as Father. He is patient and kind, not angry and demanding. I allowed Him to discipline me and noticed He is long-suffering with my disobedience. I felt less judged and more loved in the way he handled me. He didn't shield me from consequences and allowed my circumstances to bring me back to His perfect will. He was shaping me from the inside out as He infused me with His character. He was willing to wait for obedience as long as I was growing to know Him progressively and more intimately. His view was eternal, and He kept that in perspective as he lovingly restrained me and drew me to Himself. I began to see discipline as a very good thing and realized the right way was whatever was effective in that moment to bring me closer to His heart.

Many Christians know God is loving, kind, patient, and forgiving, but act as though He is not. Often, the way we are treated by people in authority over us is contrary to Father's nature. Instead of being infiltrated by God's character through the example of our parents, teachers, or bosses, we are hurt and our heart becomes wounded. Since there is no perfect parent or authority, this wound is inevitable. Our beliefs and behavior reveal our faith and perspective have been tainted by Satan's lies. As we grow to know our Father personally as He truly is, these misconceptions lose their hold on our feelings and behavior.

I became less concerned with method and more concerned about shaping DJ's will to God's will. I found boundaries very effective to keep him safe, but noticed an abundance of senseless rules frustrated him. I learned his triggers and did my best to avoid them. I realized he had a deep, innate desire to control himself and chose to see this as a very good desire. I allowed God's perspective to flood my mind and realized a strong will is not necessarily a rebellious heart, so I allowed for freedom within the boundaries. He would learn to conform to cultural expectations, but first priority was his heart. We both needed to realize who he was as a child of God, and my task was to simply encourage him toward that end. If I could see DJ the way God sees him, shaping his will according to God's purpose, parenting him would become clear. In this way, I learned to recognize any unnecessary expectations and chose my battles accordingly. I kept my perspective on eternity and realized God never gives us more than we can handle. I naturally became more patient with the maturity process.

As is often the case, things for DJ seemed to get worse before they got better. He clearly had intelligence and potential to thrive in school, but he was struggling in a way that was not necessary. He picked up repetitive habits, something he started at age three or four. One year, he would constantly pull up his pants; another, it was his socks. Still another year, he became obsessed with sniffling, though there seemed to be no physical reason for it. In the first grade, he was anxious about school, so I made the decision to homeschool him in second grade.

I knew DJ was going down an unhealthy path but wasn't sure what was wrong. He would experience such intense emotion that it would inhibit him from doing normal, everyday things. He would become debilitated by fear of embarrassment. He always seemed to struggle during certain times of the year, and I called it the rainy day blues. He seemed to focus too much and then completely lose all focus to do even the simplest task. The year I homeschooled him, he voiced the words I had always suspected, "Why do I hate everything about my life?" The realization was devastating, yet empowering at the same time.

The meltdowns grew to exponential intensity. He would feel as though everything was falling apart, releasing such emotion until there was nothing left. His emotional outbursts would leave him in a fetal position on the floor. By the end of the third grade, Casey and I decided it would be best to seek professional help. As I filled out the questionnaire for the appointment, it seemed the answers came into order for the first time. My young son was fighting anxiety and depression.

The appointment with the professional ended up getting canceled, but with the realization of what DJ was experiencing, life came into focus. We made strides toward simplifying while God taught us how to create a more stable environment in our home. That year, Casey and I were in Discipleship School, and I again functioned like a conduit. I took DJ running with me and began to draw him out like God was doing with me. I shared the revelations I was experiencing with him. Slowly, but surely, he began to heal.

I encouraged him to ponder his thoughts and taught him to recognize when they were becoming toxic. We talked through his perspectives and compared them to God's. I found with great joy that DJ accepted and agreed with deep, spiritual truths. I marveled how he perceived things about life and God that most people didn't understand. He was picking up on a plethora of messages in life. With a little encouragement, he proved to be exceptionally discerning between truth and error. I trained him to throw out the thoughts that didn't line up with God's thoughts. He understood surprisingly well for such a youngster.

By aligning his thoughts with God's thoughts, DJ's emotions have come under control. Through the years, the troublesome stress reactions have occurred less and less, most, if not all, disappearing completely. With God's wisdom, we have channeled his energies into activities that have been specifically chosen for him. We have celebrated his internal drive and taught him to trust his Spirit-led conscience. He has felt safe to come to me and share his thoughts, fears, and observations. We have our conflicts, but they are laced with love and understanding. He feels valued and affirmed in his true identity.

DJ is a living testimony to the miracle of new life in Christ. God picked him off the natural path of human nature and changed the course of his life. Instead of growing into certain mental and emotional dysfunction, he is walking toward abundant life, free from his natural tendencies. Because he has been walking in the way of his new nature for so many years, not even the complication of teenage hormones has been able to derail him. Yes, we still work diligently to keep him balanced; but through our training, we trust God is teaching him to live his life pleasing to Him. In complete surrender, I believe DJ will live a powerful and successful life in God's kingdom.

This is the miracle God has for us all. Today, by submitting to the Holy Spirit, we can walk into the person God has created us to be. Hebrews 4:7 (NIV) says, "Today, if you hear his voice, do not harden your hearts." We are no longer bound by our sin nature, the fleshly part that is of this world. We not only cope with the infirmities of the flesh but also have an opportunity to overcome in Christ. We do so by yielding our soul entirely to God's Spirit, resulting in freedom and empowerment. We become a completely new person.

Father, I humbly submit to Your Spirit; have Your way in me. Grow my patience as I trust You to transform my soul, allowing me to live out of my new nature in Christ. Encourage me today, that You are with me and desire to elevate me out of my human struggles. May I follow Your Spirit into a new life.

Chapter 12

Promised Land

Toward the end of our tenure on the fourteen wooded acres, the Lord began to speak to my heart about the Promised Land. It was never God's intention for the Israelites to remain in the desert. He wanted them to experience the abundance of Canaan, the land "flowing with milk and honey" (Exodus 33:3 NIV). Just as God led the Israelites out of the desert into Canaan, I believed God would lead us out of the wilderness and into a land of abundance. I believed this would mean a relocation for our family.

There are physical and spiritual components to God's promises. The Promised Land was a physical manifestation of God's spiritual promise of a future in heaven. When the Israelites moved into Canaan, spiritual truth became reality on earth. They took hold of the promises of God as a tangible proof of future salvation. Like Moses at the top of Mount Nebo, I was on a mountaintop overlooking the Promised Land. In a spiritual sense, I was on the edge of glory and experiencing what Martin Luther King, Jr., explained in his 1968 speech, "I've Been to the Mountaintop." He said: "I just want to do God's will. And He's allowed me to go up to the mountain. And I've looked over. And I've seen the Promised Land."

"Enjoy this while you are here," God said one day on a walk. He opened my eyes to see a glorious sight—brilliant sun rays filtering through the trees causing the flowing creek to sparkle radiantly. I knew God was encouraging me to enjoy the present and also hinting at a glorious future.

"North," he spoke on another occasion. I knew we would be moving north. He continued to encourage me for a year or so, but I did not know when He would bring this promise into reality. During this time, I poured my energy into fixing up the house for sale. I trusted God's promise and prepared for it.

In late February of 2014, Casey and I attended a banquet for a financial campaign to raise money for a church building project. During the banquet, our Pastor announced plans for a future campus to be planted north of the main campus! We were sitting with some people who had just sold and bought a new house in a bold step of faith. I asked about their realtor and found the realtor's daughter was also sitting at our table! We could see God's hand and believed we had received our commission.

This was a very exciting time for me especially, and we planned to meet with the realtor that week. Falling in love with the husband and wife team, we put our house up for sale early spring. It was not long before I realized seeing a promise through to reality was a marathon not a sprint. No one came to look at our house. The ones who did were clearly not our buyers. In addition, plans had changed within church leadership, and the northern campus was put on hold. Summer passed and the children started school. I thought we were off the hook and waited for our contract with the realtors to end.

Toward the end of the summer, a sweet young couple came to visit the house. It seemed promising, but we didn't hear from them again for a couple weeks. The Lord began to whisper that this was the couple, the one He was sending. But they didn't seem too excited. They moved much slower than I would have expected. They visited twice and then wanted to bring their parents. Like Sarah in the Old Testament (Genesis 18:12), I laughed.

My unbelief revealed itself again. When the offer came, it was much lower than I expected, and I doubted its viability. We had made a lot of updates and improvements to the house since we bought it, and I was hoping for a return on our investment. Our realtor encouraged me, saying the offer was consistent with the market. She admitted she felt we paid too much when we bought the house. We knew it was true. We had made some mistakes when we moved to Ohio, and paying too much according to the market was one of them. I thought God would bless us abundantly anyway, but He said, "I will not pass your mistake on to them." He was referring to the young couple wanting to buy the house. He was asking if I would trust Him.

We had gone back and forth with the buyers and were at a stalemate. It was a real test for me. Would I shrink back in fear and greed, or would I obey the Lord? I told my husband I thought we should take the offer, and he smiled. He knew it was true but knew I needed to come to the conclusion myself. I'd like to say after this my faith was strong, and I relied on the promises of God. But like the disciples after Jesus died, I lost hold of hope. Despite all I had been through with the Lord, despite His undeniable presence in my life, my faith failed. I doubted God's promise and at times wanted to give up, thinking it was all just a dream.

When we accepted the offer on our home, I was comforted by the prospect of buying a house I thought was to be ours. We knew a family who was fixing up a house and they were getting ready to put it on the market when ours finally sold. It seemed the timing was coming together, and I felt like all signs were pointing to this end. I thought God was preparing this house for us. But when the time came, the price was pushed out of our reach. I felt Satan had stolen it from us! "Why would you let Satan steal our house?" I accused the Lord. He was silent.

My faithful friends tried to encourage me, but I couldn't receive it. I thought it was going to end badly and felt as though the Lord had dropped us. In a last ditch effort, we put an offer on another house, but it seemed they suddenly realized they didn't want to sell their home! We were looking at the very real possibility of needing to store our belongings and move into an apartment. We were less than 30 days from our closing date.

Jude writes in verses 20–21 (ESV), "But you, beloved, building yourselves up in your most holy faith and praying in the Holy Spirit, keep yourselves in the love of God, waiting for the mercy of our Lord Jesus Christ that leads to eternal life." To build yourself up in your most holy faith means to allow the Holy Spirit to encourage you according to God's faith. This can come through the Word, through other people, or through the quiet whisper in our spirit. Many are so discouraged that they simply cannot receive the Spirit's encouragement, denying the opportunity to remain in God's love and follow Jesus into new life today.

Soon after the failed attempt to buy another home, our realtor called when I was out with a friend. She had found a house that was getting ready to be put on the market. My friend and I were close so we drove past. I had driven by this home hundreds of times while driving to and from school. When I saw it, I said, "Oh, I like that house. I like it a lot!" My friend agreed.

I went to view the house that night with the realtor. When I crossed the threshold, and saw the beautiful wood floors, I knew I wanted it. Touring the home just confirmed my initial reaction. A couple days later, Casey saw it, and we wrote an offer they couldn't refuse! But there was a catch, we needed possession at closing. Would they be able to do it?

They were willing. It was a crazy plan, but our realtor assured us this was a common practice. A chain of closings needed to happen in one day, and we were at the end of the chain. I was not naive enough to believe everything would go perfectly. Indeed, our closing was delayed, and we scrambled to find an available mover. We did our best to ensure things would run smoothly, but it was an unrealistic plan.

You would think God would make everything go your way when you walk in obedience. At least, I thought so! I had to remind myself God's priorities and focus were not mine. I also remembered how hard and long it was for the Israelites to conquer the Promised Land. In this broken world, there are troubles, and trouble we had. The movers were very dishonest. They did a beautiful job when we were watching, but we had to leave in order to attend our closing. When we returned, they were nowhere near to being finished. We were alarmed! The house was no longer ours, and we had given the new owners possession. We scrambled to honor the deal, but there was nothing to be done. The movers finished, and we had to leave before having a chance to clean up the mess. I offered to come back in the morning, but they declined.

The movers admitted they took a break and reduced our bill slightly. But as time passed, we realized the movers' break wasn't the only thing broken. The couch was ripped, a file cabinet was destroyed, the ping-pong table was damaged, a corner cabinet glass was broken, the piano (an antique and family heirloom) had a new gash, and a drawer to our desk had been ripped off. I felt ripped off. The owner and general manager of the moving company came and did what they could to make it right. But I felt wronged. And to top it all off, I got really sick during the move. I couldn't even find the medicine for relief!

Although Satan tries to bite our heels, his head is already crushed (Genesis 3:15). In Christ, Satan has no power to control or influence our lives; Christ has overcome the world (John 16:33). When we realize this in the reality of our own life, it frees us to hold on to hope. All our needs are supernaturally met, and nothing can take that from us. This means that though our circumstances might fall apart, we enter into and remain in a place of rest with the Father. Jesus says, "I am the resurrection and the life. He who believes in Me, though he may die, he shall live. And whoever lives and believes in Me shall never die" (John 11:25–26 NKJV). Satan tries to destroy our earthly life in an effort to kill our spiritual life. But this is not possible. We are Christ's and are invited into the security of the Holy of Holies, God's inner sanctuary where His very presence lives.

While the Israelites wandered in the desert, God instructed them to build a tabernacle, or tent, where He dwelled among them. Within this tent, there was an inner room where His glory rested. No ordinary man could enter, and the Holy of Holies was separated by a thick veil. Because of Christ's sacrifice, the veil was torn. We are the tabernacle, and our hope lies within that veil. No longer are we separated, and we are anchored in God's presence within our spirit.

If we can see our trials as a purification process, we will learn the secret to the abundant life. The only secret is that it is right here, right where we are, despite our circumstances. God wants to use our situation to sever our flesh from our spirit. Hebrews 4:12 (NLT) says, "For the word of God is alive and powerful. It is sharper than the sharpest two-edged sword, cutting between soul and spirit, between joint and marrow. It exposes our innermost thoughts and desires." As He exposes our flesh, the Spirit guides us into a higher spiritual life.

Over the next year, every time I saw the broken items, or worked to fix them, I prayed God would protect my heart. It was just stuff, but why did God allow it to be mistreated? I was letting go—letting go of all things temporal, letting go of money and possessions, and allowing God to save my soul. I allowed Him to save me from anger and bitterness. I was letting go of the fear that said we wouldn't have enough.

Most of our belongings were hand-me-downs and well-worn. It was time to release the scarcity mentality and move into an abundant mentality. The spirit of the world feeds on scarcity. Underlying this frame of mind is the idea of "not enough." It is characterized by fear and anxiety and causes us to feel protective about what we have and competitive about what we want. In my case, it caused me to save, save, save. I was afraid to let go of any possession because this mindset told me I wouldn't have enough for the future. I hated spending money, and the need to save money was feeding greed. I had no problem tithing or giving money to those in need because I had been well-trained by the church. But this mentality was robbing me of joy and a generous heart. I wasn't spiritually free to give because deep down, I was afraid I wouldn't have enough.

There was no need for the scarcity mentality to dominate my life. Money had become the lens through which I viewed my decisions. The abundant mentality God was leading me into is based on the idea of "plenty" in God's economy and can only find its balance in Christ. Jesus said in 2 Corinthians 12:9 (NIV), "My grace is sufficient for you." This new mentality doesn't rely on enough money, but on God to be enough. It meant trusting God more than money. Having enough money is a by-product of finding sufficiency

in Christ, something that is added as a blessing when our focus is on His kingdom. Money is temporal, and I needed to change my focus from money to God. He was freeing my mind from being consumed by everyday concerns to focus on the eternal. As long as I obeyed the Spirit's promptings when handling our money, there was no need to worry or control our finances. I learned the importance of finding my personal worth and security in Him, and this took the stress out of making financial decisions. His focus is on the eternal, and He wanted me to think eternally in all of my dealings. Whether in plenty or need, He was teaching me to find my sufficiency in Christ and put my expectation on God to provide enough. I found great peace in this perspective and began to loosen my grip on our finances.

The truth is that He had better things in mind for us, but if we held on to what we had, we couldn't receive what He was giving. The time had come for us to buy new belongings. This was God's house, and like the tabernacle (Exodus 25:9), He wanted it to be properly furnished. In a bold step of faith, we bought a custom couch. It was round and fit our new space perfectly. I hoped many family and friends would gather in our circle to encourage and love one another. The piano is part of the circle, a special touch that brings me great joy.

As time passed, I realized the location of the new house is very strategic. It is on the edge of the county and provides a gateway into the land our church has a dream to influence. A small group of Christians with a similar vision have begun meeting in our home. The piano is used by the Holy Spirit during our meetings to prepare and minister to hearts.

Appropriately, the house is located in the middle of farm fields. Abundance in the Bible is often characterized by harvest. Throughout history, God has been revealing His plan for salvation of mankind. In the Old Testament, God established annual Holy Days to celebrate the harvest seasons. One of these festivals was called the Feast of Harvest (Exodus 23:16). During this festival, the first fruits were celebrated from the spring grain harvest in ancient Israel. In the New Testament, this festival is known as Pentecost and is associated with the coming of the Holy Spirit (Acts 2:1–4). When Jesus rose from the grave, He was considered the first fruit because He was the first of God's children to be raised from the dead (1 Corinthians 15:20). Now, we also are considered first fruit when we are adopted as a son or daughter of God and experience the first fruits of heaven as a foretaste by the power of the Holy Spirit (Romans 8:23). Watching the farmers harvest their crop is a reminder that God is harvesting people for eternal life in His kingdom. We are a part of this harvest.

God continues to illustrate His plan for redemption in His people. As we allow Him to renew our minds and open our eyes to spiritual realities, we can see these tangible expressions in our own life. We realize we are part of God's story, and He uses our circumstances to illustrate His story. These manifestations become hope that we can actually grasp. This is powerful! Tangible hope naturally gives us full assurance and strong encouragement to believe God. We begin to enjoy our life in an unusual way, realizing our inheritance even now.

The writer of Hebrews powerfully proclaims hope as a steadfast anchor within the veil of God's presence (Hebrews 6:19). The end of chapter six describes how God uses an oath to prove His promise. Isaac served as a pledge of God's promise to bless and multiply Abraham's people. Even though Abraham never lived to see the fulfillment of God's plan, he knew without a shadow of a doubt God's promise was true. Something subjective became objective through Isaac's miraculous birth. The writer describes how God provides these tangible expressions to show us more convincingly the

reality of our hope. Grace and salvation was promised in the Old Testament, and Jesus became the oath when He died for us. These oaths confirm us in our faith and serve to cause us to experience God's love and favor in a palpable way.

About midway through our first year of living in the new house, I had a stunning realization. This house is my most favorite house I have ever lived in! It fits our family perfectly. I would not have picked a ranch, but with the split bedrooms and a wonderful great room in the middle, it is just right. We each have our own space, and we love the extra living room in the partially finished basement. I'm amazed because we didn't have any time to reason or think. We just bought it! God knew better than ourselves what we would enjoy most. This house has become a pledge of what is to come, something we can physically hold that gives us confident assurance of abundance and a future in heaven. By these tokens, we know God as Emmanuel, or God With Us.

In this life, we will experience heartache and pain. We may be touched by disease or devastating circumstances beyond our control. Jesus told his disciples in John 16:33 that they would have trouble in this world, and it remains true today. How is it that we can live life abundantly amidst so much pain? The answer is hope. We grieve with hope, we suffer with hope, and we heal with hope. Romans 8:28 (NIV) says, "And we know that in all things God works for the good of those who love him, who have been called according to his purpose." As we trust this promise in our everyday life, we find great encouragement to stand firm in our faith.

Proverbs 13:12 (NIV) says, "Hope deferred makes the heart sick." I am reminded of those moments, sitting on the piano bench, when my deep desires were denied. Unanswered prayer or prolonged healing can be such an affliction that it is like a chronic disease. But when we tune our ears to hear the

quiet whispers of our Father, He lifts our eyes and encourages us with the truth. While one dream may be broken, our true desires have the opportunity to rise into reality. He intends for us to experience all spiritual blessings, and He knows the way to abundant life.

Jesus prayed in John 17:15–16 (NIV), "My prayer is not that you take them out of the world but that you protect them from the evil one. They are not of the world, even as I am not of it." His prayer is that we may have eternal life, and His definition of eternal life is to know God (John 17:3). Jesus' prayer is that we would be one in Him just as He is one with God. Through oneness we experience the full measure of Jesus' joy (John 17:13).

Knowing this, we can understand and agree with God's perspective. If we know He is interested in faith, we can see our hard times as a way of letting our faith arise. If we know He is interested in trust, we can see our difficulties as a way of depending more fully on Jesus. We no longer feel the need to spend our resources on seeking a way out of our present suffering, but rightly put our energy toward seeking The Solution. We release control and trust Him to lead us out of the wilderness in His way and according to His good purpose. God is interested in eternal things, and 1 Corinthians 13:13 lists faith, hope, and love as eternal. Hope takes the focus off the immediate reality and places it in the ultimate reality. Jesus is interested in leading us into life in all its fullness. This life is beyond temporary adversity. This hope is beyond ordinary.

If we know Christ's suffering, then we can recognize and realize His joy when God's glory is revealed (1 Peter 4:13). Every single one of us becomes a living testimony of God's great love and salvation. When we walk out our personal purpose and mission, we know true fulfillment, just as Jesus did at the cross. What is more, we experience resurrection and restoration in Him and receive power through the Holy Spirit. Because of the Holy Spirit's presence in our life, we have "a foretaste of glory divine" ("Blessed Assurance" by Frances J. Crosby). God's revealed glory is the first installment of heaven, ever increasing our trust in Him. Because of these physical expressions of God's spiritual kingdom, like the Israelites in the Promised Land, we are able to have and hold hope. Confirmed hope enables us to experience life abundantly. Our new reality is an extraordinary one.

And now, "May the God of hope fill you with all joy and peace as you trust in Him, so that you may overflow with hope by the power of the Holy Spirit." (Romans 15:13 NIV)

Lord, renew my faith in You daily. Give me the courage to believe You in everyday life. May my life be an extraordinary one!

Questions for Reflection

Chapter 1

1. Why is it important for us to experience God's kingdom while still on earth?
2. How do you live life according to the Holy Spirit? If you are not sure, ask God to teach you.
3. Why is it important to believe we now have Christ's righteous nature?
4. If we have been given Christ's nature, is it valid to continue to think about ourselves as sinners? Why is it important to come into agreement with God and believe we are saints? Ask God to reveal the motivation behind your thoughts.
5. Read 2 Corinthians 5:17 and underline "in Christ." Ask the Lord what it means to live in Christ and what that looks like in your own life. Jot down your thoughts.

Chapter 2

1. When you read or study the Bible, are you allowing the Holy Spirit to search your heart and soul? Ask the Lord to reveal Himself to you personally through the Word.
2. Read Colossians 3:1–17. Reread it in another version to hear a fresh perspective. To set your mind on things above means to dwell on the thoughts and priorities of God. Pray through these verses, writing a personal devotion to God in your journal.
3. Do you feel a sense of guilt in any area of your life? It could be about work, your role as a spouse or parent, or an overall feeling of not being good enough. Ask the Father where these feelings originate, asking Him to reveal His thoughts about the guilt you feel. Dwell on what you believe God is saying, remembering that God is looking at you through the lens of Christ's forgiveness.
4. How does walking in God's forgiveness free us to forgive others? Is there a connection between our ability to forgive others and our acceptance of Christ's forgiveness? Ask yourself, "Is there someone I am refusing to forgive?"

Chapter 3

1. Why is it so important to believe the faith God puts in our spirit?
2. How does faith shape your experience in this world?
3. How does believing God's promises lead to abundant life?
4. How do you let your faith express itself in everyday life?
5. Ask God, "Father, is my faith willing, innocent, and pure?" How has the enemy's lies tainted your faith? Dwell on each and write down what you believe God is speaking to your heart.

Chapter 4

1. Are you trying to prove your faith or are you allowing God to prove your faith? What is the difference?
2. Are you allowing the difficult circumstances in your life to purify and empower you?
3. How is worry related to unbelief? When we trust God, what happens to our anxieties?
4. What might be the purpose of your own internal struggles?
5. In what way is God training you through your trials?

Chapter 5

1. Have you stopped and listened to God long enough to hear Him call you by name? Ask the Father what His purpose is for your life. (Be patient, remembering God reveals these things through time and experience.)
2. How have you felt God's confirmation in your life?
3. Is God whispering something to your heart that is different from what you have heard in this world? Ask Him for clarification and the faith to believe Him.
4. How might God be testing your calling?

Chapter 6

1. How has your perspective on holiness changed after reading this chapter?
2. Has comparison and performance distracted you from true holiness?
3. Pray, "Father, is the religious spirit stealing my abundant life in Christ?" Let the Holy Spirit open your eyes to the condition of your heart.
4. How does learning to hear God's voice in our spirit enhance our walk with God?
5. How can you become better acquainted with God's thoughts and learn to recognize His voice more clearly?

Chapter 7

1. Ask the Lord, "Father, is there any area where I believe the spirit of the world more than You? Are there any barriers in my relationship with you?"
2. Find a solitary place to quiet yourself in the Lord. Allow Him to minister to your heart. Soft worship music may be helpful to calm your body and soul.
3. Ask the Lord, "Father, in what area of my life am I doubting Your truth?" Let God speak through your spirit and through the Bible.
4. Does fear have a grip on any area of your life? Allow God to speak to your fear. Pray, "Lord, help my unbelief."
5. Is guilt and shame stealing your abundant life? Release any guilt you may be feeling and instead fill your mind with God's Word.

Chapter 8

1. How is the Lord growing your understanding of what it means to be obedient? Do you understand God's will as something you do for God? Could it be that the "way of righteousness" (Proverbs 12:28 NIV) is actually something for us? How is His will a pathway for you to experience abundant life?
2. How might your view of the Father be distorted as a result of wounds from your earthly dad? Allow the Holy Spirit to purify your perspective of God the Father.
3. In what way is fear driving you to control certain areas of your life? What are you afraid of giving up? Why?
4. How can you personally surrender to God's control and discipline? Is there an area in your life where God is calling you to submission?
5. Ask the Lord to reveal Satan's lies that are driving you to fill a need with an idol.

Chapter 9

1. In a quiet place, turn on a song of worship and truly worship God in spirit and truth, in your inner and outer self. Open your hands as a representation of your open spirit, ready to receive what God has for you.
2. After the song, quiet yourself to hear what God is speaking to you. Journal your thoughts and meditate on His (spoken) Word. Dwell on the things He has brought to mind.
3. Ask God to fill your imagination with a picture of who He sees in you and what you are doing in His kingdom.
4. Ask God to open your eyes and ears to see and hear heavenly realities. Allow Him to nurture these gifts in you over time, being patient with the process. Resist the temptation to become discouraged if this doesn't happen immediately. Simply surrender yourself to God's timing, believing Him to reveal these things.

Chapter 10

1. Ask, "Lord, am I missing out on your miraculous power due to unbelief?"
2. In what ways might you be explaining away God's supernatural involvement?
3. Faith is perspective. How might God be calling you to view your circumstances differently?
4. Faith is conviction. How might the details of your life be distracting you from your faith?
5. Submit to the Father's ways, praying, "I want to walk on water. Please show me how."

Chapter 11

1. Do you believe you can walk out of the infirmities of your flesh by walking in the Spirit and your new nature?
2. It is important to note everyone is different, and God walks us into freedom using different means. This could be through medicine, counseling, diet, or any other earthly method. What is God telling you regarding your own struggles?
3. How has God been changing your belief regarding your personal condition on earth? Do you believe He can help and even free you personally from your own difficulties? Do you believe He will?
4. Consider 2 Corinthians 12:1–10. Like Paul, be thankful if God does not remove your infirmity. Write a letter of gratitude for how He is saving you through your weakness.

Chapter 12

1. How have you experienced the kingdom of God in your life? Jot down specific blessings that are tangible reminders of your future inheritance.
2. Is it worth it for you to seek God with all of your heart, soul, and strength (Deuteronomy 6:5 NIV)? Do your priorities reflect this belief or are you excusing yourself because you are just too busy?
3. What is the "secret" to abundant life? How is it experienced here on earth?
4. Are you experiencing an abundant life? Why or why not? Let God speak into Your life, allowing Him to recreate your reality with His words. Then, believe it and walk it out in everyday life.

About the Author

Lisa Young is wife to Casey and mother to DJ, Holly, and Isaac. Between making lunches and carting kids to various activities, she is passionate about studying God's Word and worshiping Him with her whole being. She seeks to reveal God in everyday life through writing, speaking, and encouraging others according to God's personal purpose for their life. She serves at Rivers Crossing Community Church in Mason, Ohio, where she is a teacher in the Discipleship School and communicator in Next Gen Ministries.

CPSIA information can be obtained
at www.ICGtesting.com
Printed in the USA
FFOW02n1452210118